THE AVAILABILITY OF RELIGIOUS IDEAS

LIBRARY OF PHILOSOPHY AND RELIGION

General Editor: John Hick, H.G. Wood Professor of
Theology,
University of Birmingham

This new series of books will explore contemporary
religious understandings of man and the universe. The
books will be contributions to various aspects of the continuing dialogues between religion and philosophy,
between scepticism and faith, and between the different
religions and ideologies. The authors will represent a cor-
respondingly wide range of viewpoints. Some of the books
in the series will be written for the general educated
public and others for a more specialised philosophical or
theological readership.

Already published

William H. Austin
THE RELEVANCE OF NATURAL SCIENCE TO
THEOLOGY

Ramchandra Gandhi
THE AVAILABILITY OF RELIGIOUS IDEAS

Hugo A. Meynell
AN INTRODUCTION TO THE PHILOSOPHY OF
BERNARD LONERGAN

Dennis Nineham
THE USE AND ABUSE OF THE BIBLE

John J. Shepherd
EXPERIENCE, INFERENCE AND GOD

Robert Young
FREEDOM, RESPONSIBILITY AND GOD

Further titles in preparation

THE AVAILABILITY OF RELIGIOUS IDEAS

Ramchandra Gandhi

BOOKS
10 East 53d St., New York 10022
(a division of Harper & Row Publishers, Inc.)

© Ramchandra Gandhi 1976

First published 1976 by
THE MACMILLAN PRESS LTD
London and Basingstoke

Published in the U.S.A. 1976 by
HARPER & ROW PUBLISHERS, INC.
BARNES & NOBLE IMPORT DIVISION

ISBN 0-06-492324-X

Printed in Great Britain

To Indu and Leela Gandhi

Contents

Preface

I wish to acknowledge my great indebtedness to Professor John Hick. At various stages of writing this book I had the benefit of his advice and encouragement, without which I would probably not have been able to complete this work at all.

I also wish to thank Mr Satish Arora and Mr T.C. Jain for help received in preparing the typescript of the book.

An earlier version of the first chapter in this book was read as a paper at a seminar at the Indian Institute of Advanced Study, Simla, and is likely to be published in their transactions.

RAMCHANDRA GANDHI

Introduction

In this book I have brought together a number of essays on a variety of topics in the philosophy of religion: the idea of a soul, the relationship between morality and theistic prayer, immortality, the notions of the mystical and the miraculous, and so on. Although each essay stands more or less on its own, together they form a unity of approach which is more implicit than adequately exhibited in any one of them. By way of introducing the themes with which the essays deal, I should like here to spell out the nature of the unity which holds them together.

In a fundamental sense, the proper location of religious ideas can only be in the life of particular religious communities, in the communal consciousness of these communities. An exploration of the internal complexity of the consciousness of particular religious communities can be a richly rewarding philosophical exercise. And such an exercise can be undertaken both *internally,* i.e. by members of religious communities, and also *externally*, i.e. by non-members who have an imaginative access to the life and thought of a religious community. But the results of such an exercise are bound largely to fluctuate between philosophically illuminating affirmations of faith and philosophically illuminating anthropological remarks or theses. And these are important philosophical gains. To use a phrase of Whitehead's, they liberate us from what might be called the 'fallacy of misplaced concreteness' in relation to religious ideas. However, I think it would be a pity if religious ideas were not available to philosophical reflection in other ways as well. Indeed, I think they must be available to philosophical reflection in diverse ways. For even within the thought of religious communities, these ideas have crucial philosophical roles: e.g., to allay philosophic doubt, to resolve metaphysical conundrums, to articulate cosmological visions, and so on. In this way, religious ideas have always had a community-transcending capacity. This must be the explanation, or one important explanation, of how it is that religious ideas have so intricately become a part of the reflective thought and vocabulary of people who do not actively, or at all, participate in the religious life of any community. Like a magnet, philosophical curiosity attracts to itself religious ideas whose original home is of course the complex communal life of religious communities, but which are also capable of existing in and energising the uncommitted philosophical imagination.

Take the idea of *jīva,* the idea of a soul, which is so intrinsically a part of the life of the Jaina religious community, among other religious communities, in India. It connects with very specific ways of seeing the possibility of liberation from all attachments and distractions of the world. The idea of a soul is also deeply rooted in the forms of life of Jewish, Christian, and Islamic religious communities, besides others. But the fertility of the idea of a soul is such that it reaches beyond the complexities of these forms of life and energises the mind of any philosophically reflective person who wishes, for instance, to investigate the character of the thought that one is, quite simply, oneself; or the thought that one is a unique being, distinguishable from *everything* else in the world; or the thought of death as the annihilation of oneself, and so on. I imagine that it is possible to attend to these questions without self-consciously, or at all, bringing into focus the idea of a soul. But if the idea of a soul has become assimilated into one's reflective vocabulary about oneself and others, then one cannot investigate these questions without bringing them under the general rubric of the idea of a soul. One would hope that an investigation of these questions would illuminate the obscure, but powerful, religious idea of a soul — and also attendant religious doctrines, attitudes, etc. connected with the idea of a soul, e.g. the doctrine of immateriality, or the doctrine of immortality. Conversely, one would hope that careful attention to the idea of a soul, and surrounding religious views, would lend perspective to any inquiry into such philosophically puzzling thoughts as that one is, quite simply, oneself, a unique being, not any *kind* of being, and so on, which I mentioned above. In the light of what I have just said, we might want to define the philosophy of religion, or one essential aspect of it, as follows. We might say that one is doing philosophy of religion when one seeks to understand the character of philosophical problems in relation to dominant, fundamental, religious ideas, and vice versa. This is not the only way of doing philosophy, or the only way of understanding religious ideas. It is that mode of doing philosophy, and understanding religion, which rests on the assumption, the faith, that philosophical reflection and religious ideas are available to one another in a mutually illuminating way *outside* a context of actual or imaginative participation in any religious form of life, and *unconnected* with any philosophical-anthropological programme of understanding the character of types of religious consciousness. It is in this sense that the essays making up this book are essays in the philosophy of religion, and their formal unity derives from this fact.

In the first essay, entitled 'What is it like to be a human being?', I disabuse myself of the notion that inward experience, introspective or meditative, can furnish an answer to the philosophical-religious question 'Who am I?' or the question 'Who are we?', or that it could clarify the nature of the concepts 'I', 'You', 'He', etc. (The Indian mystic Ramaṇa Maharishi taught that spiritual salvation was to be gained by persistently inquiring into the character of the question 'Who am I?). Inward experience can do nothing of the kind because *being a human being* or *being myself* is not an experience of mine to which I have an inward access, and which I can understand by comparing and contrasting it with other experiences of mine. It is tempting to suppose that in self-consciousness we have a most intimate grasp of what it is *like* to be ourselves, in the way in which a man may have an intimate grasp of what it is *like* to be a sick man or an old man. But I argue that self-consciousness is a mode of being, not a mode of knowing, and that the character of the concepts 'I', 'You', 'He', etc., can only be grasped in philosophical analysis. I distinguish the question 'What are we like?' — to which natural-biological-social-scientific answers can be made available — from the question 'What are we?', which is really a question about the character of the concept 'we', and calls for a conceptual inquiry. In this way I prepare the ground for an account of the idea of a soul — the idea expressed by the personal pronouns, and this is the task I set myself in the second essay, entitled 'Soul'.

There is at the core of self-consciousness a massive conviction of self-identity. But only when this conviction of self-identity is explored further in a certain direction, does it generate the idea of a soul. The main thrust of the second essay is that the idea of a soul is *the idea of that as which we imaginatively see one another in acts of addressing one another.* When you address me, or rather, *in* addressing me, you identify me. You *mean* me. I am in no doubt that you mean me, and therefore I am in no doubt that you identify me. But in addressing me, in establishing communicative contact with me, you identify me non-referentially, non-descriptively, non-predicatively. In order for you to be able to refer to me in conversation with me, in order for you to be able to think of me descriptively or pre-dicatively, in order for you to be able to see me as a certain sort of creature in conversation with me, you must already be in a conversational relationship with me — this is a tautology, but it has an important consequence. *In* addressing me, *in* seeking a conversational relationship with me, you cannot refer to me. And yet you identify me, *mean* me! You are able to do this only because in order to be able to address me you are obliged to see me as a unique but bare particular, as *me*, and not as a creature of any sort, and in addressing me you put across to me this thought of me as myself, a soul. I suffer the profound experience of being regarded, not as a certain sort of creature, but as myself, a soul, a unique but bare particular; not a material or immaterial being, but, quite simply, as myself. I am summoned. I come forth as myself. And in self-consciousness, in the privacy of soliloquy, I imaginatively recreate this experience of being regarded as a soul. This is the basis of the massive conviction of self-identity which we find at the heart of self-consciousness, and not any introspective experience. No wonder empiricist philosophers have failed to find in their inward experience any substantival reality which they could identify as their soul. Similarly, when I see a third person as a personal subject, I imaginatively see him as the object of an act of addressing, mine or somebody else's, i.e. imaginatively *see him as being seen as a soul.* The idea of a soul is the idea of me, you, him, and all other subjects — personal subjects — seen non-predicatively, i.e. as in an act of addressing. I do not see you as of the *nature* of a soul. In addressing you I see you as yourself — a unique being. There is something redundant about the thought 'You are a soul'. The communication-establishing thought 'you' is itself generative of the idea of a soul. The religious idea of the immateriality of the soul has to do with the fact that in seeing you as yourself, as a soul, I do not see you as some*thing* — a certain kind of thing — but as some*one,* as *you.* I do not see you as a *something,* but not a *nothing* either (see Wittgenstein on Sensations, *Philosophical Investigations*, 304). Strictly we should speak not of the immateriality of the soul, but of the mode of non-substantival seeing of one another which is the seeing of one another as souls.

The ground of application of our idea of a soul is an act of addressing. Now an act of addressing has significant moral, and not merely metaphysical, features. In addressing you I seek, solicit, a communicative response from you, I do not merely causally interact with you. And I cannot solicit a communicative response from you —

thereby in some decisive sense leaving it to you to respond or not — without exhibiting minimal care for you (I may of course be unaware of all this). Thus in so far as I think the communicative thought 'you', I minimally value you, and this amounts to the same thing as regarding you as being minimally valuable, for, if I could regard you as not being valuable at all, I should be able to think the thought 'you' and yet not cast you as the object of my minimally caring attention. And this I cannot do. Similarly, in thinking of a third person as a person, I regard him imaginatively as the object of a minimally caring communicative attention, and so again as being minimally valuable. And I cannot think the thought 'I' without casting myself as the object of another's caring communicative attention. If I could regard myself as not being valuable at all, I should be able *not* to cast myself as the object of an act of addressing. But if my analysis of the complex act of the imagination symbolised by the expression 'I' is correct, I cannot do this. Thus I am obliged to regard all persons as being minimally valuable, as unconditionally deserving minimal care. This is the beginning, as I see it, of moral wisdom and the foundation of morality. And unconditional minimal valuation admits of no degrees. I cannot in rational argument *convince* anybody that he is intrinsically less valuable than myself. This is a secular version of the view that in God's eyes all men are, intrinsically, equally valuable.

I develop this theme in Essay 4, entitled 'Theism, Non-theism, and Morality'. After attempting to show that it is possible to provide a non-theistic foundation for morality, I go on to argue that, nevertheless, in limit-situations, e.g. when men are suffering beyond endurance and dying or dead, the non-theist is under an obligation to employ the language of theistic prayer. For the non-theist, like everybody else, is obliged to regard all human beings as being unconditionally minimally valuable, i.e. as possible objects of acts of addressing, acts which render them self-conscious. In view of this, how can he acquiesce in their despair and death? He must wish that there were a God as the objects of whose resuscitating act of addressing he can see the dead and the dying, and so continue to be able to regard them as minimally valuable. But what is it to wish that there were a God? It can't mean that one has discovered that there isn't, as yet, a God, but that one wishes that there would come into being a God! To think thus would be hopelessly to misunderstand the logic of 'God'. God is conceived as a necessary being. In Essay 3, entitled 'Hoping and Wishing', I argue that wishing has the character of exploratory communication. In wishing that it would be the case that p, I think the imperatival-optative thought 'If anyone is willing and able to make it the case that p, let him do so!'. Now I feel that imperatival-optative thinking necessarily has the force of exploratory communicative activity, however dim and doomed to failure this may seem. If this account of wishing is correct, then the non-theist could regard his wish that there were a God as an act of exploratorily addressing God by exploratorily addressing a help-soliciting imperative to him. As it were, he would wish that God's reality would become available to others and to himself. He would, exploratorily, call upon God to call upon others and himself. (I have the notion of what the mode of God's communicative revelation must be like. I have only made very peripheral incursions into theology in these essays.) The non-theist would need no grounds for believing in the reality of God and his resuscitating power in order to be able to address him exploratorily. He would merely have to satisfy himself that the idea of God is not a demonstrably self-contradictory idea. He would then be under a moral obligation to exploratorily, and yet un-ambiguously, employ the language of theistic prayer in relation to others. He might pray as follows – 'God, if you are there, make your saving power available to him!' But this too would have the force of an exploratory act of addressing God. Even a hypothetical help-soliciting imperative has to be, at least exploratorily, addressed to an appropriate audience or possible audience. And the non-theist need have no philosophical inhibitions in employing the language of theistic prayer in relation to himself.

In Essays 5 and 6 I investigate the notions of the mystical and the miraculous. Here again my general philosophical intention is to show the availability of these religious notions to philosophical reflection. I believe there are several notions of the mystical. There is the notion of the totality of all actual and possible states of affairs which is implicated with the notion of any particular set of actual and possible states of affairs. And yet nothing at all — nothing descriptive — can be said about the totality or system of all actual and possible states of affairs, for such a totality must be inclusive of all objects of description. The notion of the totality or system of all actual and possible states of affairs is a notion of the mystical — an essentially incomprehensible and yet ineliminable notion. So is the notion of absolute nothingness, which is implicated in every affirmative existential judgement to the effect that something, *as opposed to nothing*, exists. Again, the essentially incomprehensible notion of disembodied existence is tied up with, for instance, the utterly unmystical-seeming thought that one is alive. 'I am alive' seems an almost banal judgement. And yet consider its contradictory, 'I am not alive'. This proposition plunges one straight into the mystical idea of disembodied existence. And there are also other notions of the mystical to which I draw attention in Essay 5.

Given that the idea of absolute nothingness is not a demonstrably self-contradictory idea, and given that something exists, we are immediately enabled to form the idea of something coming into being from nothing — this is the idea of the miraculous I seek to explore in Essay 6. I argue that non-instrumental actions (what A.C. Danto has called 'basic actions') admirably fit the above description of the miraculous. Moving one's limbs, thinking, imagining, seeing, etc., are all non-instrumental doings. We are not intelligibly able to connect them with any anterior causality. They can be seen as the coming into being of something from nothing. Not what we do or think or feel, but *that* we are able to do and think and feel anything at all, is miraculous. I reject 'manipulative' accounts of the miraculous.

In the 'Conclusion', I point out that underlying all of the essays of this book is a rejection of what might be called 'the immanentist view of the world and human life'. This view expresses itself in the following, and related, forms: 'This world is all that there is'; 'This life of mine, terminated by my death, is all there is of "me" '; and so on. I argue that the immanentist view of the world and human life is unacceptable not because it is a demonstrably false philosophical view, but because it is essentially unintelligible. Once the immanentist view is rejected, a whole range of religious ideas become available to any uncommitted seeker after the wisdom of religious thought and language — e.g. the ideas of soul, God, immortality, thesmystical, the miraculous, and so on. The availability of religious ideas is the central substantial theme, and not merely the title, of this book of essays.

The central philosophical conviction which sustains practically the whole of this book is that in the most fundamental sense of the word 'given', what is given for philosophical reflection is the communicative form of human life. Self-consciousness itself is an imaginative recreation of the communicative form of human life. And morality is wholly derivative from principles of caring inherent in the communicative situation. Modifying a saying of Whitehead's, I should like to say that religion is what a man does with his self-consciousness, not his solitariness. In self-consciousness we discover the possibility of exploratory communication, the possibility of calling upon God without being under an obligation to first establish his reality. We discover the possibility and legitimacy of agnostic prayer.

A word about the problem of evil. In so far as the theistic problem of evil is intractable, the theistic consciousness must be burdened with a profound agony and despair. And in so far as the non-theist must share with the theist crucial parts of the latter's religious language, he must share this agony and despair. And theistic clarifications of the problem of evil must inevitably enrich his moral imagination. But the non-theist faces a 'problem of evil' of his own (I have dealt with this question in Essay 4). If my analysis of self-consciousness is correct (see Essays 2 and 4), then the non-theist, like anybody else, must regard all human beings as being unconditionally minimally valuable. Now if he is an evolutionary humanist, or materialist, or naturalist, the non-theist must believe that it is Nature which has generated beings — self-conscious human beings — who must logically necessarily regard themselves as being unconditionally minimally valuable. The very same Nature which is altogether too often very far indeed from being even minimally hospitable to them (men suffer beyond endurance, and for no fault of theirs or anybody else's!) So here, for the non-theist, is an apparent incoherence at the very heart of the nature of things — quite completely analogous to the logical and moral embarrassment with which the problem of evil confronts the theist. The non-theist may seek to resolve *his* logical and moral embarrassment by invoking the idea of a complex evolutionary 'strategy'. He may say that the very fact that men do not find nature unfailingly hospitable to them makes them fall back upon one another, makes it inevitable for them to adopt an increasingly humanist, co-operative, form of life. And he may seek to understand all this in terms of evolutionary strategy. But the following question remains: is a humanist, co-operative, form of life anything like adequate for dealing with the agony and despair which we suffer at the sight and thought of humanly unredeemable human suffering? The answer to this question must assuredly be in the negative. I think it is at this point that the non-theist, if he is not to become an absurdist, must examine the logical and moral and metaphysical importance of theistic language. Conversely, those theists who, despairing over the intractability of the theistic problem of evil, abandon their faith and become, say, evolutionary humanists, must realise that what awaits them is an equally intractable problem — the non-theistic problem of evil. But if my arguments have been at all sound, a flight from cognitivist theism can never amount to an abandonment of the language of theism. And the non-theist's conversion to the language of theism cannot be a merely comfortable, anxiety-allaying, conversion. For logically prior to his conversion, he is acquainted with the non-theistic problem of evil; and in participating in theistic language, he must inevitably participate in the anxiety-laden inquiry into the theistic problem of evil.

1 What is it Like to be a Human Being?

Questions of the form 'What is it like to be such-and-such?' are not always significant questions. The following, for example, are not significant questions: 'What is it like to be a planet'?, 'What is it like to be a mountain?', 'What is it like to be a prime number?' Why are these questions non-significant? These questions lack significance because, for a question of the form 'What is it like to be such-and such?' to have significance, it is essential that being such-and-such should involve having experiences on the part of whatever it is that is such-and-such; and because being-a-planet, being-a-mountain, being-a-prime number, does not require that certain configurations of matter or certain numbers should have, or be capable of having, experiences of any kind. I shall, however, presently argue that for a question of the form 'What is it like to be such-and-such?' to have significance, it is not sufficient that being-such-and-such should involve being-an-experient.

Consider some examples of questions of the above form which are significant questions: 'What is it like to be a pilot?', 'What is it like to be a father?', 'What is it like to be a prime minister?'. Why are these questions significant questions? Clearly they fulfil the condition that being-such-and-such should involve being-an-experient. But they also fulfil, and reveal, another crucial condition. For a question of the form 'What is it like to be such-and-such?' to be a significant question, it is essential that whatever is such-and-such should not *only*, or *merely*, be such-and-such. If a person is a pilot, he is not only, or merely, a pilot; if a father, then not only, or merely, a father; if a prime minister, then not only, or merely, a prime minister. What the fulfilment of this condition ensures can be brought out in the following way. If a person is a pilot, but not only, or merely, a pilot, then he can compare and contrast his being-a-pilot with other actual or possible modes of his existence, e.g. being-a-father, being widely-travelled, etc., and he may find, and we may agree with him, that there were some experiences of his which illuminatingly tie up with his being-a-pilot. In this way we could expect from him, or on his behalf, an illuminating answer to the question 'What is it like to be a pilot?'. The questions 'What is it like to be a father?', 'What is it like to be a prime minister?', also fulfil this condition, and thus achieve significance.

Consider now some difficult questions of the form 'What is it like to be such-and-such?'. Take the question 'What is it like to be a child?' Weary of our grown-up-ness, we may ask this question. But we cannot ask a child this question. A child lacks anything like an adequately self-conscious experience of modes of being other than the mode of being-a-child, so he cannot illuminatingly tie up any of his experiences with his being-a-child. We have no alternative but to observe children carefully, rummage through our childhood memories, exercise our imagination, and in this somewhat indirect and inauthentic way hope to reach an answer to the question 'What is it like to be a child?'. The question 'What is it like to be woman?' would similarly require great perspicacity and alertness to the subtle and elaborate roles that women play, and are constrained to play, in human social and sexual life, if it is to be at all satisfactorily answered. An unhappy man may ask 'What is it like to be happy?' and find it very hard, and so may others, to say what feeling or network of feelings, if any, crucially ties up with being happy.

Consider the question 'What is it like to be a dog?'. Is this a significant question? Can we imagine what a dog's experiences are like? Perhaps we could imaginatively try and fix in our mind some such experience as a dog's experience of being hungry, angry, etc., understanding the quality of these experiences on some inevitably stretched analogy with parallel human experiences. At best such an exercise would yield only feebly plausible results. But *this* is not why the question 'What is it like to be dog?' is a non-significant question. This question is non-significant because we cannot say — nor could a dog, assuming it was gifted with a capacity for philosophical reflection — *which* of a dog's experiences were illuminatingly tied up with a dog's being a dog. A dog, or for that matter a man, is always and only and merely a dog or a man. It is no good trying to say, for instance, that in addition to being a dog or a man, a dog or a man is something 'beyond' a dog or a man. For this something 'beyond', if there is such a thing, would be built into the idea of a dog or a man. Similarly, if it is asserted that in addition to being a dog or a man, a dog or a man is something 'less' than a dog or a man, one could insist that this something 'less' should be built into our idea of a dog or a man. But then we would again have to say that a dog or a man — our idea of what a dog or a man is having now been enriched or rectified in the above ways — is always and only and merely a dog or a man. And we would not be able to find among the experiences of a dog or a man some experiences that were distinctively the experiences of a dog or a man, and others that were not.

Let us now stop this pretence of being able to talk about a dog's experiences with authority and confine ourselves to human experience. All the experiences of a human being are the experiences of a human being. We may for certain purposes exalt some experiences and downgrade others, but *qua* human experiences they are all logically on the same level. It isn't only our experiences of love and hate and tragedy and peace that are human experiences, so are our experiences of hunger and thirst and boredom and fear. There must be something distinctively human about all human experiences — this is a necessary truth. We can't say that our experience of hunger must be indistinguishably like a dog's experience of hunger, whereas our experience of love and hate is distinctively human. Our experience of hunger and thirst, precisely because it is *our* experience of hunger and thirst, must bear the stamp of our distinctiveness. And it is no

less a human experience than any other experience of ours.
So we cannot call to mind some of our experiences, to the
exclusion of others, and say '*That* is what it is like to be a
human being'. Nor can we call just *any* human experience
to mind, or any indefinite number of human experiences,
and say '*That* is what it is like to be a human being'. We
cannot contrast any of our experiences with non-human
experiences, and yet this is what we must be able to do if
we are to answer the question 'What is it like to be a
human being?'. And among human experiences we cannot
in logic dignify some as being more distinctively human
than others. It looks as if we cannot answer the question
'What is it like to be a human being?'.

Strictly speaking, the question 'What is it like to be a
human being?' can only be addressed to a being who is
capable of being, perhaps 'becoming' is the right word
here, various kinds of being, including a *human* being. We
shall have to imagine here that there is a pure consciousness or spirit which successively assumes a canine,
feline, and human form, and so on. Assuming continuity
of memory, etc. we could speculatively say that such a
consciousness would be able, through recall or imaginative
contrast, to answer the question 'What is it like to be a
human being?' in the way in which a human being could
answer the question 'What is it like to be a child?' and
similar questions. But the metaphysic underlying this
hypothesis is contrary to the spirit of the would-be
significant question 'What is it like to be a human being?'
For *this* question is the same as the would-be significant
question 'What is it like to be what we are?', which is not a
question about some state or mode or condition of
ourselves.

I have just spoken of the questions 'What is it like to be
a human being?' and 'What is it like to be what we are?' as
would-be significant questions. They are not, of course,
significant questions. The question 'What is it like to be a
human being?' is mistaken to be a significant question
because we construe it on the analogy of such questions as
'What is it like to be a child, an old man, a sick man, a rich

man, a poor man, etc.?' A human being is not a human being in the way he can be a child, an old man, a sick man, etc. It does not make sense to actually inspect, or imaginatively grasp, the quality of the experiences which, allegedly, tie up significantly with a human being's being a human being. There can be no such tie-up, every human experience being, as I argued earlier, as distinctively human an experience as any other human experience. It makes good sense, of course, to actually inspect or imaginatively grasp the quality of the experiences which illuminatingly tie up with being a child, an old man, a sick man, etc. The non-significance of the question 'What is it like to be what we are?' is also fairly obvious. We are what we are, and cannot, in logic, be anything else. Consequently there is no inward contrast available to us between a mode of being which is 'our' mode of being and a mode of being which is not our mode of being.

The non-significance of the question 'What is it like to be a human being?' has an important consequence which can be brought out in the following way. Somebody might say the following:

The sciences — natural, biological, social — have made available to us a vast storehouse of information about human beings and their modes of existence, about the forms and structure and processes of development of their social organisation, and so on. Nevertheless, all this information, perhaps it should even be called knowledge, pales into insignificance when it is contrasted with the qualitatively utterly distinct and unique and special understanding each one of us has of what it is like to be a human being. We not only *are* human beings, we are self-conscious creatures, we have an immediate and inward acquaintance with what it is like to be human being. And this acquaintance, it should be called knowledge, is not, unlike scientific knowledge about human beings, of an inherently fragmentary kind. Our grasp of what it is like to be a human being is of its nature holistic. One could say that self-consciousness fills the space of our being, although it is constantly developing. A man's inward understanding of what it is like to be a human being, unlike scientific knowledge about human beings, may not enable him to predict and control the course of human affairs, including the course of his own life, in any remarkable way. Nevertheless it is only the former, and not the latter, kind of knowledge that constitutes authentic understanding of a human being.

If my arguments so far have been sound, the whole of the above diatribe is shot through with misunderstanding. Nothing, not even our inward experience, exceptional or everyday, can be an answer to the question 'What is it like to be a human being?', because this question is a spurious question. To say this is not to deny the reality or to question the importance of subjectivity and inwardness in human life. Although our inward experience cannot constitute any sort of answer to the senseless question 'What is it like to be a human being?', there *are* questions of the form 'What is it like to be such-an-such?' to which answers can only be given by an appeal to inward experience. Consider the following questions: 'What is it like to be a child?', 'What is it like to be an old man?', 'What is it like to be a sick man?', 'What is it like to be a dying man?'. Such questions can only be answered, or sought to be answered, by inspecting closely actual or imagined inward experience. But notice one thing. With regard to the kinds of questions I have listed above, crucial scientific knowledge can be made available. And there is here no desire on the part of anybody to exalt inward experience and downgrade scientific knowledge, or the other way round. The two are complementary. Take illness. A diagnostic judgement to the effect that a man is suffering from a certain disease has, in medical treatment, to be importantly supplemented by information, inwardly supplied by the patient, as to how he is 'feeling', etc. And if there occurs a worryingly painful modification of our inward experience (i.e. if we are not feeling well, to put it non-pedantically), we seek medical information about possible organic and functional disorders. Similarly it would be ridiculous to give an imaginatively rich inward account of childhood without trying to correlate such an account with the anatomical, physiological, and socio-logical peculiarities and handicaps of the condition of childhood. And so on. Our inward experience is a crucial, and often the only, guide to our understanding of various states and conditions and modifications of our being, but it does not tell us what it is like to be a human being.

Our mental lives are indeed haunted by a sense of deep and final self-acquaintance. But this fact constitutes a mode of being, not a mode of knowing, not even a mode of understanding. Self-consciousness is this mode of being. Impossible metaphysical and epistemological puzzles have arisen as a result of mistakenly construing this mode of being as a mode of knowing. Regarded as a mode of being, it becomes immediately evident why self-consciousness cannot be fragmentary, although it could be fitful or steady. If self-consciousness were fragmentary it would be *consciousness*, circumscribed by the range of its objects, and not the unitive mode of being that it is. So it is simply absurd to compare, unfavourably, the admittedly frag-mentary character of scientific knowledge about human beings with the allegedly holistic character of inward knowledge, which is self-consciousness. Self-consciousness is not a mode of knowing at all, and so the comparison completely falls to the ground.

A word about authenticity. It is only renderings of inward experience that can be called more or less authentic, downright inauthentic, and so on, because there is much room here for bogusness and self-deception. Of course scientific knowledge-claims about human beings can also be bogus, but the criteria of bogusness and genuine-ness here would be different. A 'scientistic' metaphysic on the other hand can be bogus in just the same way as a bogus rendering of inward experience, e.g. some forms of current materialism which must involve what F.P. Ramsey called 'feigning anaesthesia'.

I should like to conclude with some remarks on the questions 'What is a human being?' and 'What are human beings?'. From the spuriousness of a question of the form 'What is it like to be such-and-such?' we cannot infer the spuriousness of the question 'What is such-and-such?' For instance, from the spuriousness of the question 'What is it like to be a planet?' we cannot infer that the question 'What is a planet?' is also spurious. It manifestly is a perfectly significant question. Similarly, because the question 'What is it like to be a human being?' is a spurious question, we cannot say that the question 'What is a human being?' is also a spurious question.

When we ask the questions 'What is a human being?' and 'What are human beings?' we are quite simply asking the question 'What are we?' This is because the concept of a human being is the concept of 'ourselves', the concept of myself, you, he etc. Now with regard to ourselves, we can ask a variety of questions, such as: 'What is the nature and ancestry of our bodies?'; 'What is the nature of our forms of social organisation?'; 'What is our history?'; and so on. These are questions to which natural-biological-social-scientific answers can be made available. Crudely we can say that the general form of such questions is 'What are we like?'. This is a perfectly significant question, unlike the question 'What is it like to be what we are, to be ourselves?'. However, the question 'What are we like?' is not logically the most fundamental question we can ask about ourselves, and cannot be the logically most fundamental rendering of the questions 'What is a human being?' and 'What are human beings?'

Why is the question 'What are we like?' not the logically most fundamental question that we can ask about ourselves? Because it presupposes that we understand the concept of 'we', and the connected concepts of 'myself', 'you', 'him', etc. But do we have a clear grasp of the nature of these concepts? The fact that I am myself, and am a self-conscious being, may generate the illusion that I know inwardly what it is like to be myself and thereby possess the most intimate understanding of the concept of 'myself' or 'I'. But this illusion must be exposed and resisted, as I have tried to do in this essay. And even if this were not an illusion, no inward experience is going to enable us to grasp the concepts of 'you' and 'him'. As a matter of fact, it is only philosophical analysis that can enable us to grasp this whole range of concepts. Neither inward experience nor scientific inquiry can assist us here. Thus in their most fundamental sense, the questions 'What is a human being?' and 'What are human beings?' are philosophical questions.

I cannot here undertake an analysis of the concepts 'I', 'you', 'he', etc. (I attempt such an analysis in the next essay, 'Soul'.) I shall merely make a few remarks about the character of any such analysis, and about some conclusions which I believe we are bound to reach if we undertake such an analysis. First of all, the concepts 'I', 'you', 'he', etc. can only be explicated in terms of concepts of human communication. The concept 'you' is fundamentally the concept of an audience. I cannot use the word 'you' in relation to you except in communication with you. The concept 'I' is fundamentally the concept of an imagined audience. In thinking the complex thought symbolised by the expression 'I', I posit myself as the object of an imagined act of addressing, i.e. as an audience. Similarly, the concept 'he' is the concept of a possible audience. I cannot think of him as him without positing him as the object of an imagined act of addressing, i.e. as a possible audience. Now *in* casting you in the role of an audience, I necessarily think of you non-predicatively, i.e. quite simply as 'you', and not as a certain sort of being. Not that you are not a certain sort of being, only that I cannot have the concept 'you' if I am not able to think of you non-predicatively. Thus in so far as the concepts 'I' and 'he' are also tied up with the concept of an audience, the concept 'you', we have these concepts only because we are able to think of ourselves non-predicatively, i.e. quite simply as ourselves, and not as beings of a certain short. Not that we are not beings of a certain sort, only that we cannot have the concept of 'ourselves' if we cannot think of ourselves non-predicatively. This has an important bearing on the character of the question 'What are human beings?'. For if this question is the same as the question 'What are we?', where 'we' means 'ourselves', then any satisfactory answer to this question must exhibit the following feature. It must not merely have the form 'We are such-and-such'. It must explain how being such-and-such equips us with the ability to think of one another non-predicatively, i.e. quite simply as one another, and not as being such-and-such, or anything else. The only answer capable of fulfilling this expectation is this: 'We are communicative beings.' Of course we are not *merely* communicative beings. But the concept 'we' — and our possession of this and related concepts is our most fundamental characteristic — can only be explicated in terms of the concept of communication. I do not know what else to say about the character of the question 'What are human beings?' except that there is a great deal more that needs to be said.

2 Soul

What is it to be a human soul? This is a vast question, it suggests a profound inquiry into the nature and depth and complexity of human personality, an exercise in spiritual psychology. Such an exercise is beyond my powers and is not the object of this essay. I hope in this essay merely to clarify one or two essential features of the concept of a human soul.

Talking about the self, H.D. Lewis says:

> It cannot be identified in terms of any pattern of experience or of any relation to a physically identifiable body. How then can it be known at all? It is known, I maintain, solely in the way each one, in the first instance, knows himself to be a unique being. No one, at this level, is in any doubt as to who he is — he is himself. ['The Elusive Self', in *Talk of God* (Royal Institute of Philosophy Lectures: Macmillan, 1969) p.168.]

This sense of final self-acquaintance is undoubtedly a central feature of our mental lives. Apart from knowing, and being conscious of, a variety of facts about ourselves and our situation, we are also aware of ourselves as being *ourselves*. My awareness of being myself, in the sense in question, appears not to depend on my knowledge or ignorance of facts *about* myself. There is another sense of being aware of oneself as being oneself where this would not be the case. A man sometimes says 'I do not feel myself today', and what he means by these words is that his responses, gross and subtle, of thought and feeling and will, are *not* the kinds of responses with which he is familiar, a familiarity which is a crucial part of his knowledge about himself. So there is a sense in which I *can* say 'I do not feel myself', but there is another sense in which this would be nonsense. There is, we want to say, in all self-consciousness a *conviction* of self-identity which cannot without absurdity be disowned. Of course self-consciousness itself may be lost or ruptured and the conviction of self-identity may also consequently be lost or distorted. But in so far as self-consciousness retains the lucidity of the power of thought, the conviction of self-identity cannot without absurdity be disowned. And this conviction of self-identity can survive severe loss of memory. Despite loss of memory of a kind crucial for identification, a man may ask the question 'Who am I?', thereby exhibiting an unimpairedness of consciousness which cannot exist without the conviction of self-identity.

Of course, this conviction of self-identity un-accompanied by what might be called adequate self-knowledge by description would hardly be enough for *self-confidence*. It is not a cheerful experience — the conviction of self-identity, merely, without benefit of memory of public identity. Yet it is crucial for under-standing the concept of a human soul — that is of our conviction of a deep and final, although elusive, self-acquaintance.

This conviction of self-identity is not reducible to knowledge *that* one is so-and-so, such-and-such, or even that one is *really* so-and-so, such-and-such. It is not an *experience* of self, but a conviction of self-identity. One could say that it is the conviction of *Advaita,* of not-being-two-or-more, to put it negatively, and of being-oneself, to put it positively, which is both a conviction of being-one, and of being oneself. Thinking about anything can only proceed on the assumption that the thing in question is self-identical. Thinking about oneself can only proceed on the basis of the conviction that one is self-identical.

It looks as if nothing more has to be said about this conviction of self-identity. The reality of the conviction has to be acknowledged (if one is not to be 'absent-minded' in Kierkegaard's sense), and then one moves on to problems and issues connected with one's knowledge or ignorance *about* oneself. I feel, however, that this conviction of self-identity would be incompletely understood if its character were not explored further in a certain direction.

The conviction of self-identity that I have been talking about cannot be separated from the thinking of the thought symbolised by the expression 'I' or 'I, myself' or 'Me', 'Myself' etc. The conviction *is* the thinking of this thought. But what does the thinking of this thought consist in? Clearly, in thinking the thought 'I' I do not call to mind the *name* of something familiar. I do not, in self-consciousness, encounter an entity called *myself* and the thought 'I' is not an act of naming anything or recalling the name of anything. Besides, my name is R.G., not 'I'. If 'I' were, *per impossibile*, to be the name of anything, it would have to be the name of the person who was naming himself — but that would have to be the name of the person who is naming the person . . . who is naming himself. Infinite regress here. Thinking the thought 'I' is not a mental act of naming or recognising or remembering, recalling, etc., anything. But it *is* an act of some kind or other. In thinking the thought 'I' I do not assume an observational, introspective, stance. In thinking the thought 'I' I involve myself in an act. What act? *Not* an act of referentially or descriptively identifying myself or recognising myself. 'The father of L.G.' is a thought by means of which I can referentially or descriptively identify myself to others, and also recall to myself my public identity, or an aspect of my public identity. But an analysis of such an act of identification would not be an explication of the conviction of self-identity which is what I am trying to get clear about. *That* conviction is founded upon non-referential, non-descriptive, non-predicative, thinking — the thinking of oneself as being oneself. Whatever else one might be. But of this later.

What *is* the thinking of the thought 'I'? Let me state shortly what I believe to be the shape of the correct answer to this question. In thinking the thought 'I' I perform an act of imaginatively adopting an audience-stance. Before I can explain what such an act amounts to, I must explain what I mean by an audience-stance. When I am addressed by somebody, a speaker, I am *uniquely picked out, I am non-referentially identified, I am called forth* — I can use a number of such synonymous expressions to indicate what being addressed amounts to. Let me explain first what it is for me to be non-referentially identified . When you address me — whatever be the means you employ (use a descriptive phrase, or issue a vocative utterance of some other kind) — you do not, *in* addressing me, *refer* to me in conversation with me. The possibility of a conversation starting between us depends on the success of your initial addressing-act. And yet it cannot be denied that your action has a communicative force. You do not merely interact with me, you invite me to attend to you, to listen, pay attention, etc. to you. And your act has the communicative force of such utterances as 'Attend to me!', '*Listen*!', etc. That you identify me in addressing me is borne out by the fact that in addressing me you put me in possession of the thought 'He means me'. And yet you identify me without referring to me! I think this is a fact of some fundamental importance, but easy to lose sight of. The notion of identification has been on the whole understood either in terms of the phenomenon of recognition or in terms of the activity of identifying some items or other for a hearer in conversation with him. We also talk about the identification of persons along these lines, thereby ignoring the fact that there is a unique mode of identification of persons, the mode of identification which consists in addressing them or in being addressed by them. When I am addressed by you, I have no doubt at all in my mind that you mean *me*, that you have picked *me* out, and — given adequate success of the act of addressing — that you know that I know that you have identified me, picked me out. You have not, *in* addressing me, referred to me. If I seek to understand your act of addressing me as an act which amounted to your referring to me, I would not think that you were initiating communication with me at all. I would either think that you were referring to me in communication with somebody else, or that having already initiated communication with me, you were referring to me for some purpose or other. I cannot recognise your act of addressing me as an act of addressing me, if I do not see that the whole rationale of it consisted in your identifying me without referring to me, in your creating a condition which makes reference to me possible, but which does not itself involve a reference to me. In addressing me you seem to gain a special inward access to me. This is sufficiently rich to enable me to grasp that you have identified me, but because of the essentially non-referential character of your mode of identification, I feel that you have communicated to me your thought of me as myself, and not as a creature of a particular kind, but quite simply as myself.

I hope I have made reasonably clear the notion of non-referential identification of oneself in an act of addressing, in an act of being addressed by another. Now suppose one thought of self-consciousness in the following way. Suppose one regarded the thinking of the thought 'I' as an essentially imaginative act, an act of imagining that one was being addressed. Such an act of the imagination would be an act of imagining that one was being regarded simply as being oneself. It would involve imagining that one was being thought of as a unique but bare particular, a soul. Not that one *is* a bare particular, only that for an act of addressing to take place, it is essential that one imagine one's audience quite simply as himself, a unique but bare particular, and not, *in the same act*, as a creature of a particular sort. So self-consciousness would seem to have these two faces. The conviction of self-identity which pervades it would spring from an actual experience of being involved in an act of addressing, or from an act of imagining that one was involved in an act of addressing.

If *in* addressing me you had to refer to me in some way, you would be casting me in the role of somebody who is identified by some description or other, some referring expression or other. And I would merely *happen* to be the person you identified. Another person could easily, conceivably, have fitted the description. But the directedness-towards-me of your act of addressing me (whatever the conventional means you employ, and this could consist in your employing a referring expression such as, for example, 'Mr Chairman', which could conceivably fit somebody else) makes it clear that *in* addressing me you non-referentially identify me, that you transcend the referential language that you may have employed in order to address me; that you acknowledge my uniqueness. Addressing is a uniqueness-acknowledging act.

Only when I suffer the experience of being vocatively picked out do I experience my uniqueness. I am called forth — of all the things in the universe, an appeal is made to *me*. Indeed the concepts of 'I', 'me', have their seat in the experience of being vocatively picked out. We do not, through a private effort of attention or consciousness, experience our uniqueness. I think H.D. Lewis is wrong in suggesting that each one of us simply finds himself to be the unique self that he is. It is only when I am summoned, called forth, etc. that I realise my uniqueness.

I cannot acknowledge my own uniqueness. For in order to do that I shall have to acknowledge the uniqueness of myself acknowledging the uniqueness of myself . . . . Infinite regress here.

In being addressed, one experiences the uniqueness of oneself, one becomes charged with the conviction of one's uniqueness. Because one becomes conscious of being some*one*, and not merely something. A some*one* is the only kind of being who can be non-referentially, non-predicatively, identified, be thought of quite simply as himself.

Imagining that one is being addressed involves imagining that one's state of consciousness is that of one who has been uniquely picked out, called forth. I have been arguing that the conviction of self-identity which haunts our mental lives is nothing but the sense of being uniquely picked out, of being called forth, imaginatively conjured up. This conviction is thoroughly imaginative in character. It is small wonder that empiricist philosophers have failed to find introspectively anything substantival in the contents of their consciousness which they could legitimately call their self. The *self* is to be found either *actually* in an act of addressing, in one's being regarded quite simply as oneself, or *imaginatively* in an act of imagining that one was involved in an act of addressing, in which case it would be a sense or conviction that one was being regarded quite simply as oneself, and not merely, or at all, as a creature of a particular kind.

There does appear to be something attractive about Lewis's suggestion that each one of us quite simply finds himself to be the unique being that he is, each one of us finds that he is quite simply himself. But what is the nature of this *finding*? In meditation, in careful attention to myself, I do find a massive core of conviction, the conviction of self-identity. But this conviction is not a passive experiential finding. It has the disequilibrium of thought. The conviction of self-identity is the thinking of the thought 'I', it is the thinking of the thought that I am myself, or, quite simply, that I am. Now what is thinking? Are we quite clear about the nature of thinking? The conviction of self-identity cannot be regarded as being something like a sensation which is experienced, or some emotion which is suffered. It is suffused with all the tentativeness and precariousness of thinking. Just because thinking is an extraordinarily puzzling phenomenon, we cannot, despite its simplicity and attractiveness, accept the Lewis-type of account of self-identity. Thinking cannot be regarded as a mere private agitation of experience. Here I am thinking of reflective, self-conscious, thinking. There may of course be other types of thinking, but I am not concerned with these types of thinking here. Self-conscious thinking can only be regarded as an imaginative communicative interchange between oneself and an imagined other. And at the heart of this whole mode of imaginative activity is a fundamental act of the imagination, the act of imagining that one was being addressed by an imagined other. Such an act of the imagination yields the thought that I am myself, that I am being regarded quite simply as myself, and not merely, or at all, as a creature of a particular sort. Conversely, the thought that I am myself cannot be separated from the act of imagining that one was being addressed. And this act of the imagination is what generates the possibility of an elaborate imaginative activity of considering, reflecting upon, weighing up, etc., the utterances of an imagined speaker — i.e. the possibility of reflective thought. Thus I have no doubt in my mind that the Lewis type of account of self-identity is a simplistic illusion. The conviction that I am myself is not gained by attention or introspection, it is understood only in the context of an act of imaginative communication.

Only in an actual act of being addressed do I fully suffer the experience of being uniquely picked out, called forth, of being regarded quite simply as myself, of being thought of non-referentially, non-predicatively, etc., i.e. of being regarded as a soul. In a situation of being actually addressed, the thought which is yielded is the thought 'I am called', 'I am summoned', etc. The imaginative apprehension of oneself as being regarded as a soul must be a truncated experience. What I am trying to say is that the thought 'I' is a sort of incomplete version of the thought 'I am called', 'I am uniquely picked out', etc. The truncated experience symbolised by the expression 'I' may generate the illusion of an autonomous self, existing in isolation from other actual or possible selves. It may generate the illusion that one is a soul, a unique but bare particular. Whereas what ought to be said about the notion of a soul is the following: one is regarded as a soul in an act of addressing, and one imagines that one is being so regarded in an imagined act of addressing. These are self-imposed illusions without which there can be no human communication or reflective thinking. It would be a mistake simply to say that one is a soul, a non-predicative entity. The notion of a soul gets a foothold in our life because, in an act of addressing — in an act of establishing communicative contact with another — we have to imagine that our addressee is a unique but bare particular, we have to identify him non-referentially, non-predicatively. There is some danger of losing sight of the original communicative context in which the notion of a soul finds a foothold. This is the danger of the truncated thought 'I' (an incomplete version of the thought 'I am called by him', 'He calls me', etc.) yielding the unacceptable conclusion that one *is* an attributeless entity, a bare particular, that as a matter of empirical fact, one *is* a soul. But this danger can be overcome easily if we constantly remind ourselves of the communicative original ground of the notion of a soul.

I have so far talked about the notion of a soul in a rather self-centred manner. Our experience of soul is wider. When I cast another person, you, in the role of an audience ('you' arise for me in this way), I regard you as a soul — as yourself and not, or not merely, as a certain sort of creature. I said earlier that the thought 'I' constitutes a truncated experience of soul. The thought 'I am called' and the thought 'you' are full experiences of soul. They are *realisations* of (*a*) the fact that I am being regarded as a soul, and (*b*) the fact that I am regarding you as a soul. Indeed I cannot think the thought 'you' unless it amounts to my regarding you as a soul. One can say that the thought 'I' is a *visualisation*, the thought 'you' is a *realisation* ('I do not have the opinion that he is a soul, my attitude to him is an attitude towards a soul' — so says Wittgenstein in *Philosophical Investigations*, Part II). Wittgenstein's remark ought to lead one to reflect upon the thought 'he' or 'him'.

I can think of him as *him* only to the extent I posit him as the object of an imagined act of addressing him — my own or another's. My recognition of a person as a person has to do with my being able to see him as the object of an imagined act of addressing. Here, obviously, considerations like his possessing a certain sort of body, his behaviour being of a certain sort, etc., are crucial. Not every kind of being can I see as the object, actual or possible, of an act of addressing. Animals, with varying success, plants hardly, material objects not at all. But in being able to see a certain sort of being as the object of an imagined act of addressing, I cut through the details and characteristics of his being, or animal being, and see him as a soul — am able to think of him as himself, and not merely as a being of a certain sort. In thinking of him as him or as himself, I regard him as a soul, because I regard him as being capable of being regarded as a soul, i.e. his being capable of being vocatively identified. So this is another dimension of the experience of a soul — being able to regard somebody as being able to be regarded as a soul. This is what the thought 'he, himself' amounts to.

In thinking the thought 'I' I *think*. I ask myself questions, e.g. the question 'Who am I?'. But does it make sense — literal sense — to ask oneself a question? I do not think so. If self-communication were literally possible, it would make sense to literally address oneself — addressing being a necessary condition of communication. But to address oneself one would have to invite oneself to . . . invite oneself to attend to oneself. This is impossible. So all I can say is that in thinking, in what appears to be a case of asking myself questions, I *attend* to questions. And this involves *imagining* that the questions are addressed to me — i.e. that one is in communicative relationship.

Take the question 'Who am I?' which I appear to discover at the heart of my conviction of self-identity, as a question I appear to ask myself. Let us look at this in the following way. I imagine somebody (such a being can be imagined as being quite anonymous) asking me the question 'Who are you?'. This would involve my imagining that in one sense — in the sense of vocative identification — I was perfectly adequately identified, singled out, picked out, called forth. This would be the core of my conviction of self-identity. At the same time I would imagine that I was being asked to identify myself in the usual way (to give details about myself which could be checked). But knowing that I do not have to give myself these details, I would be completely puzzled as to what I am supposed to do. I think this explains the dizziness-producing character of the 'self-addressed' question 'Who am I?'

What is it to *believe* that one is a soul, you are a soul, he is a soul? The notions of oneself, you, and him are notions that capture the attributeless mode in which we must, at any level of depth, think of ourselves and one another. Here the strangeness of Hume's famous words become apparent. Hume says, 'For my part, when I most intimately enter into what I call myself . . .', and then goes on to add that when he does this he 'never can observe any thing but particular perceptions'. Now it seems to me that for a person to 'most intimately enter into' what he 'calls' himself (notice the communicative word 'calls' here) would be to grasp the structure of the act of imagination which is calling oneself 'I' or 'I, myself', and that to grasp the structure of this act is to grasp the attributelessness of the mode in which I — imaginatively — posit myself as an object of another's act of addressing. Similarly to most intimately think of 'you' is to grasp the attributelessness of the mode in which I cast you in casting you as the object of my vocative act. And to think of *him* as being uniquely him is to imaginatively see him in the attributeless mode of his coming forth in response to a vocative call.

All this is *not* to have the *opinion* that I am an attributeless but unique entity, and you and he too. For one thing, to have these opinions would be to think something *about* myself, you, him; it would not amount to *thinking the thoughts* symbolised by the expressions 'I', 'you' and 'he'. It would not be to enter most intimately into what I call myself, you, and him. So there is a general difficulty about any metaphysical *belief* about the soul. Such a belief would be incapable of grasping the sheer givenness — in imaginative or actual relationship — of ourselves to ourselves and to one another. It would seek to grasp the *what* of ourselves, when, most intimately, we are *that* we are.

In so far as I think — and in so far as thinking is imaginative communication — I cannot fail to see myself as being regarded as a soul (as myself, a unique being, and not a certain sort of creature). But is this the same thing as regarding oneself as a soul? I do not think so. I would regard myself as a soul if I could literally address myself, non-referentially identify myself. It is a profound illusion that in thinking one literally talks to oneself, addresses oneself. And it is this illusion which is responsible for the further illusion that in self-consciousness one finds oneself regarding oneself as a soul. But I cannot address myself. In order to do so I would have to invite myself to invite myself to . . . invite myself to attend to myself. And all this is impossible and absurd. So I cannot, except profoundly mistakenly, regard myself as a soul, believe that I am a soul. I necessarily, actually or imaginatively, see myself being regarded as a soul, but never see *myself* as a soul. It appears that one can only see another as a soul, or be seen by another as a soul. (But perhaps one can say that in self-consciousness one is vouchsafed a vivid thought or *idea* of oneself as a soul, i.e. as, quite simply, oneself.)

But what does seeing another as a soul come to? I address you, cast you in the role of an audience, make it possible for myself to think of you as a 'you'. I have maintained that in all this I see you as a soul, i.e. quite simply as yourself, and not as a certain sort of creature. Addressing comes off as a full-fledged act when my act of addressing you solicits your communicative attention — as it were your readiness to enter into a communicative relationship with me. It is this 'coming forth' of you which is the basis of my thought of you as a 'you'. All referential, predicative, thinking falls away when you respond with communicative attention to my act of addressing you. I cannot even say that I am *confronted* by you. The situation of communicative arousal is such that I cannot point towards you in communicatively arousing you. I cannot indicate to you or to myself the presence before me of any sort of substance. The impossibility of pointing, reference, necessitates this. And yet I acknowledge you as a 'you', prompt you to attend to me communicatively. This is action at a distance, an action which has a target, but no origin. The idea of the immateriality of the soul has its root here, I think. Non-referential identification cannot at the same time be descriptive of any condition of materiality. This is not to say that in addressing you I see you as an immaterial substance. I do not see you as any sort of substance, because if I did, it would be possible for me at the same time to think of you referentially or predicatively. But this is not possible. I see you as a person, a unique being, not as a substance – a thing. I do not wish to imply that persons are queer sorts of things. What is to be emphasised is that involved as we inescapably are in the human communicative form of life, we are obliged to interpret communicative behaviour, attention, in a certain way: as disclosing a non-substatival reality of inwardness and personality – a metaphorical non-spatial *centre* of the living human body. Such a centre is 'you' as the object of my act of addressing, 'he' as the object of an actual or imagined act of addressing of somebody else's. And the thought 'I' has the consequence of my imagining that I was such a centre for an imagined other.

If 'you', 'he', and 'I' were names of substances, material or immaterial, I should never be able to think of you or him non-referentially, non-predicatively, and never be able to imagine that I was being so thought of. But I am, in addressing you and in seeing him and myself as objects of imaginative acts of addressing, able to think in this style. This is a disproof of the substantival view of 'I', 'you' and 'he'. I am not in saying all this displaying gross absent-mindedness about the human body. We find ourselves as involved in communicative forms of activity. And this involves the interaction of living human bodies: we do not communicate with dead bodies. Notice, that in saying that we do not communicate with dead bodies I am deliberately shirking the issue of 'communication' with the dead, with spirits. What we hear and read about such 'communications' does not amount to the kind of reciprocal encounter which is the mark of communication between living human beings, and which itself has to be set against a background of a whole mode of co-operative activity and form of co-operative life of human beings

which, in the case of spirit-phenomena, is manifestly
absent. An isolated question-answer phenomenon, however
oddly 'accurate', cannot be described as a communication
because of the lack of such a background. The living
human body and the animation of human interaction are
essential to get the phenomenon of human communication
going. Of course there has to be a transcendence of a
merely interactionist mode of operation for there to be
communication. In addressing you I do not merely attract
your attention to myself — I make it clear to you that I
was 'not really' merely attracting your attention to myself,
that I was inviting, soliciting, your attention. But if there
weren't an initial capacity for attention-attraction, there
could be no act of deliberate sacrifice of this capacity with
the consequence that the attention of one's would-be
audience is not merely elicited, but solicited.

In the light of what I have been saying above, I should
now no longer want to say that I am in any sense
conscious of myself as being myself. The conviction of
self-identity which pervades my mental life is not an
experience of oneself as oneself, but the unavoidable
discovery of oneself as the object of an imagined act
whereby one is seen as a soul by an imagined other. The
unavoidability of this imaginative experience — in so far as
one is self-conscious — is what generates the illusion of an
actual immediate acquaintance with oneself as oneself.
(But I think one can think of self-consciousness as vouch-
safing not an experience, but a powerful picture of oneself
as a soul).

In his *Lecture on Ethics* Wittgenstein mentions that one
of the quite unaccountable feelings he seems to have is
that of being *absolutely safe*, and he thinks that this
feeling has something to do with the recognition of the
dimension of the ethical. Just as the feeling — or rather the
query — as to why there is anything at all, and not
nothing, has to do with the dimension of the mystical. I
think the account of the notion of a soul which I have
been developing can throw light on this thought of
Wittgenstein's.

I have argued that the sense of deep and final self-acquaintance which haunts our mental lives is to be understood as the thinking of the thought symbolised by the expression 'I'; and that this thought has to be understood as an act of the imagination, an act of imagining that one was being addressed, vocatively picked out. In so far as I remain self-conscious, in so far as I think the thought 'I', I must unfailingly perform the above act of the imagination. *Being* self-conscious is for me the *same as* performing this act. (Barring the case when I am rendered self-conscious by being actually addressed by somebody). Now an act of addressing, say your act of addressing me, has significant moral, and not merely metaphysical, features. In addressing me, you exhibit the fact that you *minimally care* for me, you exhibit minimal concern for me. I do not mean by this that you express the least possible concern for me, but rather that you express concern for me which cannot fall below a certain lower limit. It *has* a lower limit. For an act of addressing, if it is to be an act of *soliciting,* and not merely an act of trying to *elicit*, a communicative response from an audience, must be *minimally respectful* of the would-be audience's freedom — it must be in some decisive sense *left to him* to respond communicatively or not. If this is not a real option for him, the would-be act of addressing, be it couched in the most conventional forms of an act of addressing, will in reality be a merely causally efficacious, and not a communicative, act. In view of this fact there remains something profoundly paradoxical about a communicative act which consists in a speaker trying to disown all concern for the well-being of his audience. In so far as he addresses his audience — this he must do in order to enter into any sort of communicative relationship with him — a speaker acknowledges his minimal concern for his audience, and it is only self-stultifyingly that he can go on in the same breath to try to disown all concern for his audience. (But is this *ethical* concern? Can I not, at the same time as regarding you communicatively, intend to destroy you because, for instance, I believe that you are so

evil that only your destruction can save mankind? And if
this is possible, then it would appear that I do not, in
regarding you communicatively, necessarily regard you as
being minimally valuable. I consider this difficulty in Essay
4, p. 65.)

Now I am not always being addressed by another
person, so I cannot say that I am always undergoing the
experience of being minimally cared for. But in so far as I
am or remain self-conscious, I unceasingly imaginatively
set myself up as the object of an act of addressing, i.e. as
the object of a minimally caring attitude. To be self-
conscious is to imagine oneself as minimally cared for.
Thus in so far as I am lucidly self-conscious, I must feel
absolutely safe, i.e. such that I cannot completely fall
away from concern and care.

In the same way when I address somebody, I exhibit
minimal care towards him; and I can seek to deny this only
on pain of self-stultification. And also when I think of a
third person as a person, as I have argued, I necessarily
imagine him as being the object of an act of addressing. I
thus necessarily imagine him as being minimally valued. I
logically necessarily cannot fail to imagine or regard
myself, you and all others, in so far as I think of them as
persons, as being minimally valued, minimally cared for. In
this way I see communicative creatures as being under a
grace which cannot, so long as they are self-conscious, fail
them. There is, as it were, an environment of caring all
around communicative creatures.

What about what appear to be non-communicative
creatures? Do they not have souls? Here I think the nature
of animal life demands to be understood in a certain
crucial way. I think that although we do not communicate
with animals with any degree of adequate reciprocity, the
animal character of their life, and the approximation of
that life to the animal character of our life, is such that I
can imagine them as being objects of an act of addressing.
Not perhaps of a familiar human act of addressing; but of
an infinitely more loving consciousness, or a very much
more loving consciousness than the average human con-

sciousness — if not God, then Saint Francis. I can imagine animals being cast in the roles of communicative respondents — being regarded as souls. But there has to be an element of fantasy here — but not illegitimate fantasy. Animal life of all types can be seen as having a centre — not only neurophysiologically, but also behaviourally. The idea of a soul is the articulate notion of such a centre. This centre turns out not to be a spatial centre but a communicative heart, a soul.

If my account of the nature of self-consciousness is correct, then it becomes possible to understand that feeling which every communicative creature has of being a special creature. This has to do with the experience of being uniquely picked out, of being regarded as a soul. (The idea of a chosen people. The entire class of communicative creatures, *specially picked out*, vocatively identified, chosen in this sense.)

In imaginatively responding to an imagined act of addressing, I do *not* identify, even imaginatively, the addresser. Although I must think of the addresser as being a person, I do not embody him, or see him or picture him or imagine him as embodied. On the other hand, my experience of being vocatively picked out, which is at the root of my conviction of self-identity, is an experience of finding not that one is *not* embodied, but rather that *one* is embodied, that there is a centre— this can only be metaphorically understood — to the animal organism one is — a soul. One sees oneself as being regarded as such a centre. There is no denial of spatio-temporal physical location; there is a discerning of an 'inside' to a certain region of physical reality.

So it appears that, for self-consciousness, it is indispensable that I imaginatively respond to an imagined act of addressing, but unnecessary to imagine an embodied addresser. I think connected with this is the idea of an unembodied caring consciousness under whose protection all creatures live — a minimally caring consciousness. Not located anywhere, but present everywhere where there are communicative creatures.

An unlocated unembodied caring consciousness can also
be seen as a pure caring act — act of loving summons — the
bringer-forth of souls.

There is no difficulty in seeing that I cannot intelligibly
conceive of my own death — the ceasing to be, for good,
of myself — my consciousness. I can conceive of temporary lapses into unconsciousness, always overcome by a
return to consciousness, but not an inherently irreversible
unconsciousness. The difficulty is this: in asking myself
the question 'What will it be like to be irreversibly
unconscious?' (and the state of affairs here sought to be
visualised would exclude all dream activity and dream-
thinking of all types), I want both to remain self-conscious
and visualise actual loss of capacity for self-consciousness.
This cannot be done. In the light of the preceding
discussion we can see that what I want to visualise here is
this: I want to visualise a condition where it would not be
possible for me to *come forth*, actually or imaginatively, in
response to a vocative call. But the condition in which I
try to visualise this is a condition of *coming forth*,
imaginatively, to such a call. I cannot, self-consciously,
conceive of myself as being unresponsive to communication. My very act of conducting such an experiment
is an instance of my responsiveness to an imagined act of
addressing.

Similarly, I cannot conceive of *you* as not being —
inherently incapable of being — responsive to communication. In conceiving of *you* as *you* I have already
successfully cast you in the role of a communicative
respondent, solicited from you a communicative response.
Or at any rate I have successfully imagined you as coming
forth in response to my call. I cannot go on thinking of
you as you and at the same time try to imagine you as
being incapable of being 'you'. I cannot *both* call you
forth and try to see you, at the same time, as not being
capable of being called forth.

In the same way, I cannot try to conceive of him, so
long as I am able to think the thought 'him', as being
incapable of being a communicative respondent. In thin-

king the thought 'him' I have already successfully imagined him as an addressee.

But surely I can fail to think the thoughts 'you' and 'he'? If people around me started dying I would be incapable of casting anybody in the role of an actual or imagined addressee. Indeed the notion of 'anybody', because the notion of 'others', would cease to be available to me.

Similarly, if I am dying, slipping into what I would, without intelligibility, be constrained to take to be irreversible unconsciousness, the notion of *myself*, or the notion of *I*, would *begin to cease* to be available to me. There would be a growing incapacity to think the thought 'I' − or any other thought, such as the thoughts 'you' or 'he'. The result of this would be an increasing failure to cast oneself imaginatively as an addressee, as an object of minimal care. I think this is the horror of dying − the realisation as it forces itself upon one that one has been or is being forsaken ('My God, my God, why have you forsaken me?').

And the horror of the death of others, that one cannot, even minimally, care for them, that one has forsaken them, that one does not have the power to revive them, to call them forth (Jesus askes Lazarus to *come forth*). There is a powerful picture here. One has the feeling that one does not have the love and the power to revive, to call forth, that one is unequal to the task of saving. So one imagines an infinitely loving and powerful being who brings forth and calls forth the dead and the dying. One is under an obligation to imagine this, in so far as one does or would love one's fellows.

I used to think that the obligation of well-wishing only enjoined that one wish that one's fellows would not be obliterated by death. This is so, I think, but for this wish to have substance one would have to imagine an infinitely loving and powerful being summoning the dead and the dying by means of a suitably efficacious and adequately loving act. They must first be resuscitated and then come forth.

Thus to wish the dead and the dying immortality or even survival is at the same time to wish that there were a God.

There is something odd about the thought 'I wish there were a God'. The thought carries the implication that I have found that there is not — as yet — a God. This is nonsense — it amounts to seriously misunderstanding the logic of 'God'. The wish should really be that one be able adequately to conceive of and so believe in (this is the whole of the ontological argument) God.

A wish of the form 'I wish that it would be the case that *p*' has the force of the imperatival utterance: 'Anybody who is able to and willing to make it the case that *p*, let him make it the case that *p*!' Let us try and understand on this model the wish 'I wish I could adequately conceive of God'. Such a wish would have the force of the imperatival utterance, 'If anybody can and would help me adequately to conceive of God, let him do so!'

Let us ask: who can such an imperative be addressed to? To superior beings, saints, gods? (There is a whole theory of subordinate deities here.) I haven't thought at all clearly enough about the significance of poly-theistic language. So I won't pursue this question here. But why can't one imaginatively call upon God to call upon one? (And why only *imaginatively*? The idea of God is not, I believe, a demonstrably self-contradictory idea. And it is the idea of a communicative being. So I can *really*, although exploratorily, but not merely imaginatively, communicatively seek God and his care.) One has to think this perhaps: let the imagined minimally caring being who calls me forth into self-consciousness be disclosed as a *real presence*, in reality, and not merely imaginatively, there. This would involve communicatively looking for God by invoking him. It is logically in order to look for a communicative being, in whose reality one has no *grounds* for believing, by seeking to address him. What the mode of God's communicative revelation must be like, I have no idea. I have only been doing minimal theology in this essay.

3 Hoping and Wishing

I often change my mind in the course of development of this essay, but in a clarifying, I hope, and not a merely disavowing manner.

I

What is the difference between hoping and believing? One cannot say: 'I believe that p, although I have not done very much, directly or indirectly, in the way of acquainting myself with evidence for the truth of "p".' But one *can* say: 'I hope that p, although I have not done very much, directly or indirectly, in the way of acquainting myself with evidence for the truth of "p".' However, perhaps one cannot say: 'I hope that p, although I have done *nothing* in the way of acquainting myself with evidence for the truth of "p".' Could one say: 'There must be some basis for hoping that p, but "grounds for hoping that p" need not be as strong as "grounds or reasons for believing that p" '?

II

The very fact that I say that I hope that p and not that I believe that p indicates the relative weakness of whatever evidential support there is, if there *is* any, for my hope that p, compared to the strength of the evidential support that would be required if I were to *believe* that p.

III

But does this mean that hoping is merely 'weak' believing? This cannot be the whole story. Weak believing would express itself in other forms: e.g. in the form of the following expressions: 'I am inclined to think that p', 'It seems to me that p', 'I have the feeling that p', and so on.

IV

There seems to be an extra element in hoping. Perhaps this is wishing. And perhaps wishing is part of hoping because of the latter's weak evidential support. I will return to this point later.

V

Consider again the suggestion that hoping is 'weak believing'. I think one could argue against this suggestion in the following way. One can say that while hoping that p certainly does involve a *look* at evidential considerations of a kind which would incline one to think or believe that p, there is also involved in hoping that p a tacit acknowledgement of the existence of evidential considerations which would incline one to think that *not-p*. Hoping necessarily goes hand-in-hand with fearing that what is hoped for may not turn out to be the case. This being so, one cannot speak of 'grounds for hoping' at all. Because then there would be a mutual cancelling out of grounds for hoping and grounds for fearing. And this antagonism would not generate a residue of probabilistic expectation. For if there were such a residue, one would say, not 'I hope that p', but 'I am inclined to think that p', or something like that. Perhaps the locution 'I am hoping that p' does connect with the notion of 'grounds'. But I do not think this locution in any way centrally illuminates the phenomenon of hoping; so I shall not consider it further in this essay, beyond drawing attention to it here.

VI

Although *hoping* is not at all like believing, it is a phenomenon which is suffused with inductive considerations. This is what makes it difficult to see its true character. For instance, it seems to me a necessary condition of my hoping that p that I or somebody else should be able in principle to specify the general nature of the *kinds* of conditions that would have to be fulfilled for it to be the case that p, and also the general nature of the kinds of conditions the fulfilment of which would bring it about that *not-p*. It would, for example, be odd for me to say 'I hope that it rains this evening, although I cannot, even in principle, nor can anybody else, specify the general nature of the kinds of conditions that would have to be fulfilled for this to be the case'. It is in this respect that hoping differs from pure wishing. For me to wish that it would be the case that p it is *not* necessary, although often it would be possible, that I, or anybody else, should be able, even in principle, to specify the kinds of conditions the fulfilment of which would bring it about that p. Wishing lacks the kind of inductive context that hoping necessarily requires.

VII

Difference of context apart, there is a very close relationship between hoping and wishing. One can argue that my hoping that p involves a double-act of wishing. An act of wishing that the conditions that favour the coming into being of the state of affairs represented by 'p' *would* obtain, and also an act of wishing that conditions that do not favour the coming into being of the state of affairs represented by 'p' would *not* obtain.

VIII

Perhaps an analysis of my hoping that p into a double-act of wishing together with a specification of the inductive context of my hope would be a sufficiently perspicuous analysis of my hoping that p.

IX

In spite of what I have said above, I think it is the case that the notion of hoping is often used in the sense of 'weak believing'. When a doctor says, about a patient, that his condition is not hopeless, what he means is that there *are* grounds, although not strong, for thinking or suspecting that the patient may pull through. The doctor, *in* saying that the condition of the patient is not hopeless, does not wish that the patient would pull through. The doctor may even be an ill-wisher of the patient and *not* wish that the patient would pull through. I think one can say that the notion of hoping is being employed in its 'weak believing' sense when what we are confronted with are locutions, or variations of locutions, of the form 'There is hope that p'. But when we are confronted with locutions of the form 'I hope that p', then the notion of hoping that is being employed is one which lends itself to being analysed into the notion of a wish or the notion of a complex of wishes.

X

When someone says 'There is hope that p', the question, 'What are your grounds for saying that there is hope that p?', and also the question, 'What are your grounds for hoping that p?', are legitimate questions. So I was wrong in suggesting that the notion of 'grounds for hoping' has no application. It has no application only in those cases where we are confronted with locutions of the form 'I hope that p'. So we have the 'weak believing' sense of hoping as exemplified in locutions of the form 'There is hope that p' and the 'wishing' sense of hoping as exemplified in locutions of the form 'I hope that p'. Let us call these senses H_1 and H_2.

XI

When the doctor says 'The patient's condition is not hopeless', does he merely mean that there is a finite, as opposed to nil, probability that the patient will pull through? No. I think a minimally adequate probabilistic basis is essential here.

XII

When a man says in despair, 'There is no hope for me!', what does he mean? I think what he means is that even 'weak belief' that he will overcome his despair is not available to him. Of course, in sense H_2, he could still hope. He can say 'I hope I will be all right!' But notice how close such hoping is to wishing.

XIII

What is it to 'hope against hope'? When a man says 'I am hoping against hope that my friend will regain consciousness', what does he mean? Clearly he is not 'weakly believing'. Nor is he hoping in the sense of pure wishing. I think the situation is as follows. There is a finite, as opposed to nil, probability of his friend regaining consciousness and our man forms a 'groundless', 'unreasonable' (but not logically absurd) expectation of this finite probability coming off. This is yet another form of hoping. Let us call this 'sense H_3' of hoping. It is quite clear that hoping in sense H_3 would also include a strong element of wishing (wishing can be present even in hoping of the H_1 kind, but not necessarily). If I am hoping against hope that p, I am also wishing that the tiny probability which supports my unreasonable expectation would come off.

XIV

What sort of hoping is involved in religious, more particularly theistic, hoping? Say the hope that one's personality will be not obliterated by death, that the injustices of this world will be put right in another, 'transcendent', world? Let us consider various possibilities.

(*a*) Can we say that the theist who hopes that he will survive death can express his hope in the form 'There is hope that I will survive death'? This is hoping in sense H_1, i.e. the sense of weak believing. I do not think the theist can hope in this way. The doctor who says, 'There is hope for the patient', has a fairly clear notion of the general nature of the kinds of conditions (upon the fulfilment of which the survival of the patient depends) he regards as not being utterly improbable, although not bright. The theist, on the other hand, can specify no such condition whatever, conditions with regard to which there is general or specialist knowledge. (This is because of the utter imcomprehensibility of the mode of disembodied existence of consciousness, and the incomprehensibility of the process of disembodiment which, on the survivalist view, must be attendant upon the death of a person.) His hoping *is* an instance of pure wishing.

I think the point I am trying to make here can be made in another way. One could say that the availability of locutions of the form 'There is hope that *p*' requires the availability, also, of locutions of the form 'There is no hope that *p*', 'There is little hope that *p*', 'There is some hope that *p*', and so on. And what *this* presupposes is that there should be general or specialist understanding and knowledge of the truth-conditions of the proposition 'p'. Such understanding or knowledge is just what does not appear to be available when 'p' is the kind of proposition which enters into theistic hoping. Consider the propostion 'I will survive death'. Do we understand the truth-conditions of this proposition? We don't, and that is because our mode of access to the ideas of survival and annihilation is not a cognitive mode. What might be called the facts of death generate powerful pictures, but not cognitively clear ideas, of survival and annihilation. We fear annihilation and wish that we would survive death (Some people have also of course wished that they would not survive death — they have sought annihilation.) But the point is that our concepts of fearing and wishing do not *require* that the objects of fearing and wishing be cognitively clearly intelligible. Unless I am failing to see some subtle aspect of the concept of hoping, it seems to me that all hoping is unavoidably embedded in a background of inductive understanding of the world.

(*b*) Can we say that the theist hopes in sense H_3, i.e. in the sense of 'hoping against hope'? I do not think so. When I hope against hope that a friend would regain consciousness, I know that science can provide a fairly clear characterisation of the wildly improbable conditions the fulfilment of which alone can save my friend. But the theist is here again at a loss to specify the nature of the conditions upon the fulfilment of which he purports to base his 'hope against hope'. The conclusion again seems irresistible that the theist is merely wishing.

(*c*) Can we say that the theist is hoping in sense H_2? But even to hope in sense H_2 that, e.g., would be the case that *p*, requires that we should be able, at least in principle, to specify the general nature of the kinds of conditions whose fulfilment would bring it about that *p*. And this the theist cannot do. Again the conclusion forces itself upon us that the theist is not hoping at all, he is merely wishing. Wishing that it would be the case that *p* does not necessarily require that the person who wishes that it would be the case that *p* should be able to specify, even in principle, the general nature of the kinds of conditions the fulfilment of which would bring it about that *p* (although, often, such specification would be possible). But wishing, unlike hoping, does not *call* for such specification of conditions.

XV

If what I have been saying about the nature of hoping is sound, then it becomes quite clear that the theist's charge that the non-theist has no basis for hoping (transcendentally) becomes quite meaningless. Transcendental hoping turns out to be a case of pure wishing and wishing is no monopoly of theists. (But what if the theist's hope is that God would effect the *miracle* of survival, and so on? I consider this possibility in the 'Conclusion', making use of my discussion of related issues in Essays 4, 'Theism, Non-Theism, and Morality' and 6, 'The Miraculous'.)

XVI

What is it to wish that something would be the case? Notice that locutions of the form 'I wish that it would rain' *cannot* be replaced by locutions of the form 'I wish that it will rain'. I think this point is of more than mere grammatical interest. It suggests, I think, that the object of wishing is not propositional in character. 'It would happen', unlike 'It will happen', is not a proposition. For this reason there can be no illuminating comparison of wishing with believing, thinking, even hoping, etc. The notion of 'grounds for wishing' makes no sense at all.

XVII

Can we say that the force of 'I wish it were (would be) the case that p' is the same as the force of 'Would that it were the case that p!'? I think so, and this equation clearly brings out the non-inductive character of wishing. But is the form 'Would that it were the case that p!' perspicuous? Does it simply amount to the expression of a feeling of regret (that it is not the case that p) combined with the envisaging of a desired state of affairs which is represented by 'p'?

I think when I wish that it were the case that p, I do more than merely envisage, with varying degrees of clarity, a desired state of affairs. I think wishing that it were the case that p involves, necessarily, the thinking of the thought 'Let it be the case that p!'. It would be self-contradictory to assert 'I wish that it were the case that p, but let it not be the case that p!'. But what is the force of the locution 'Let it be the case that p!'? In a communicative situation, this locution would have an unavoidably imperatival force, as in 'Let this man go!'. But what is the role of the *thought* 'Let it be the case that p!'? 'Let it be the case that p!' — as a thought — is, I have suggested, the force-bearer of the act of wishing that it were the case that p. I suggest that thinking the thought 'Let it be the case that that p! can be understood in the following way. The thought 'Let it be the case that p!' can be reformulated as the following thought: 'If anyone is able and willing to make it the case that p, let him do so!'. So formulated, the imperatival character of the thought becomes immediately apparent. But how can a *thought*, a piece of unuttered language, be said to be imperatival in character? Do I, in thinking the thought 'If anybody is willing and able to make it the case that p, let him do so!', seek to address this thought — let us call it the thought 'T' — to anybody? Clearly I do. I seek to address the thought 'T' to the entire class of agents in the world, and in doing so I presuppose the possibility of telepathy. *A priori* critics of telepathy should pay attention to the embeddedness of the idea of telepathy in ordinary acts of wishing, in acts of thinking such thoughts as the thought 'T'. Whatever may be the difficulties in the way of understanding the nature of telepathy, it can hardly be denied that in thinking a thought such as the thought 'T' I reach out, exploratorily and would-be-communicatively, towards an audience who might grasp my unuttered thought and possibly fulfil the wish contained in it.

I should now like to add a footnote to my account of certain forms of theistic hoping in section XIV of this essay. I had maintained that theistic hoping appears to be an instance of wishing. This is because all hoping requires a background of inductive understanding of the world, and because no such understanding is available in relation to the 'transcendent world' which is the concern of theistic hoping. But even if this view is correct, theistic hoping is not reduced to a mere private agitation of the mind. Suppose that, as a theist, I entertain the hope that my personality will not be obliterated by death. On my account of theistic hoping, this hope of mine merely amounts to the wish that my personality would not be obliterated by death. But on my account of wishing, such a wish has a communicative structure. It amounts to my exploratorily addressing the following thought to the entire class of actual and possible agents: 'If anyone is able and willing to resuscitate my personality beyond death, let him do so'. As a theist, I would address, or seek to address, this thought quite specifically to God. My wish would be a prayer. If we see theistic hoping as wishing, and if theistic wishing is prayer, the 'groundlessness' of theistic hoping ceases to be a source of logical embarrassment.

XVIII

My analysis of the mental act of wishing would explain the *prima facie* inexplicable fact that the *mere fact* of my having a certain wish, the public avowal and attempted fulfilment of which are socially taboo, can make me feel guilty, even if I make no avowal of my wish and do not seek to fulfil it in any way. Let my wish, that it were the case that p, be such a wish. Now if my analysis of wishing is correct, my wishing that it were the case that p would necessarily involve my exploratorily-communicatively addressing the hypothetical imperative 'If anyone is able and willing to make it the case that p, let him do so!' to the entire class of agents in the world. That is to say, it would involve my imagining that I had made a public avowal of my wish. Guilt-feelings would naturally emerge. I am assuming that I would feel guilty if I made a public avowal of my wish. Given this assumption, my analysis of wishing shows that there is a necessary connection between my wish that it were the case that p and my feeling guilty.

XIX

I want to say a word about past-oriented wishing about which so far I have said nothing in this essay. We not only wish that something would happen in the present and the future, we also wish that certain things *hadn't* happened in the past. What is this latter kind of wishing? Does it merely amount to an expression of regret, sorrow, disappointment, etc. about the past? Is there no 'exploratory communication' here? I think there is. We not only wish that the present and future of mankind would not involve the evil of apparently unjustifiable suffering, we also wish that the past of mankind hadn't been so full of apparently unjustifiable suffering. And in so wishing we do not merely express sorrow or indignation. Implicit in such a past-oriented act of wishing is the following thought: 'If anyone is capable of bringing about such a state of afffairs that the past suffering of mankind (not to mention animal suffering) can be seen as not having been in vain, not having been an ultimate irrationality, let him do so!' And such a thought, such an utterance, is exploratorily-communicatively addressed to all agents in the universe, actual or possible, including God. It can plausibly be exploratorily only addressed to an omnipotent, caring, being, whose transformative capacity is unlimited beyond imagination, i.e. to God. It amounts to calling upon God, exploratorily, to accomplish the miracle of a complete transfiguration of time, including the past. I don't think we can show how all this is possible. But we can *wish* that this would happen, and so exploratorily call upon God to make it happen.

4 Theism, Non-theism, and Morality

I

Theists and non-theists alike would regard acts of inflicting harm, injury, pain, etc., upon one's fellows as being morally unjustified except under special circumstances. But their attitudes to the mere *fact* of human suffering would vary profoundly. For the non-theist, what brings about human suffering — e.g. some human action or other — may be an object of moral judgement or appraisal. But the mere *fact* of human suffering — e.g. the fact that a man is in pain — is not a proper object of moral attitudes. It is a natural phenomenon, mérely, and while one can feel pity for the man in pain, one cannot morally appraise his being in pain. Of course, the humanist — a non-theistic moralist — would regard an attitude of letting the man suffer, when his suffering can be allayed, as being blameworthy. But here he would be morally appraising a human action or attitude and not the mere *fact* of human suffering. The non-theist might of course regard human suffering as being an 'evil', in the sense of being something which we ought, in so far as it lies in our power, to reduce or eliminate. But human suffering which is *not* in our power to reduce or eliminate — that would, for the non-theist, be morally neutral. But not so for the theist. His conviction is that human beings are created by a perfectly good being, who is also omnipotent and omniscient, so that *no* instance of human suffering can be without moral justification. If only we could understand God's ways, we would see that our sufferings are not — or need not be — in vain, we would see that they fulfil — or could fulfil — some secret purpose of

God, and so are *not* morally unjustified. But human beings very often suffer for no fault of theirs — so it appears anyway — and also they suffer beyond endurance. Why does God break the human spirit in this fashion — even if he has the power to reconstruct it? Sensitive theists have worried about this problem, and they have given a name to this problem — 'the problem of evil.' This is the problem of reconciling God's goodness and omnipotence with the fact of unbearable, apparently unjustified, human (not to mention animal) suffering. The idea that such suffering has a retributivist justification, that it is morally educative, that it is an essential ingredient of a larger good, this idea has not sounded very convincing — and not only to non-theists, but also to many theists. Of course, theists believe that it is the limitation of our intellect and moral imagination which prevents us from seeing the solution to the 'problem of evil'.

For sensitive theists, the 'problem of evil' is a source of both moral and logical embarrassment. The non-theist's attitude of moral neutrality towards humanly un-redeemable human, not to mention animal, suffering, is not, apparently, a source of either moral or logical embarrassment to him. I want to argue that the fact of humanly unredeemable human suffering ought, at any rate *prima facie*, to be a source of logical embarrassment to the non-theist, especially to an evolutionary non-theist. I shall begin by presenting an argument to show that it is logically impossible for a human being, in so far as he is self-conscious, not to value himself in some sense or other, or not to regard himself as being valuable in some sense or other.

Consider the belief or thought 'I do not value myself in any sense whatever'. It can be argued — see Essay 2, 'Soul' — that the use of the symbol 'I' in thought represents a very complex intellectual act — an act of imagining that one was the recipient of an anonymous speaker's com-municative attention, i.e. an act of *imaginatively* placing oneself in an audience-stance *vis-à-vis* an imagined speaker. This is what makes thinking, which can be regarded as an imaginative listening to, weighing-up of, etc., the imagined utterances of an imagined speaker, possible. Anyway, let it be granted that the use of the symbol 'I' in thought does not signify an act of naming or referring to an immaterial substance, but represents an act of imagining that one was the recipient of an imagined speaker's communicative attention. Now communicative attention *has* to have a minimally caring characteristic. It cannot degenerate into purely interactionist activity. It must be an activity of *inviting, soliciting* responses from an audience, and not an activity of merely eliciting, *causally bringing about*, responses from the audience. If this be so, then the act of imagining that one was the recipient of an anonymous speaker's communicative attention would be equivalent to an act of imagining that one was the recipient of a minimally caring attitude, i.e. that one was valued, however minimally. One cannot self-consciously — i.e. in a way which involves the thinking of the complex thought symbolised by the expression 'I' — deny this to be the case. But one might attempt to say the following: 'I can't, in so far as I am self-conscious, help imagining that I am valued, however minimally, but I *ought not to*.' But this will just not do. The thought 'I ought not to' equally involves the use of the symbol 'I', and so the thinker of this thought must also regard himself as being minimally valued. But is this the same thing as regarding oneself as being minimally valuable? I think so. If one is such that one cannot — logically cannot — fail to cast oneself as the object of a minimally caring attitude, whenever one is self-conscious, one cannot fail to regard oneself as being minimally valuable. If it were possible for one to regard oneself as not being valuable at all, it would be possible for one not to cast oneself as the object of a minimally caring attitude. But this is not possible. Therefore, a self-conscious human being necessarily regards himself as being minimally valuable.

How would an evolutionary non-theist react to this situation? The fact that human beings logically cannot help regarding themselves as being valuable in some sense or other can be understood in terms of evolutionary 'strategy'. A being who *logically* cannot help regarding himself as being valuable in some sense or other is more likely to struggle harder for survival than some other kind of being for whom self-valuation was not a matter of logical necessity. This is obvious enough. But why should creatures have evolved who face the profound embarrassment of realising that although they cannot help valuing themselves, they are subject to a degree of suffering which makes them lose confidence in the very basis of their distinctive style of life, i.e. self-consciousness — the very characteristic which makes self-valuation a matter of logical necessity for them, and hence increases their survival-power? This is the 'problem of evil' as it arises, or must arise, for the non-theist. In so far as he is a believer in the coherence of reality, he must feel profoundly embarrassed by the fact that nature should have evolved a being who cannot — logically cannot — help regarding himself as being minimally valuable, but who is set in an environment which is far from being unfailingly hospitable to him.

I think the following response can be made on behalf of the non-theistic humanist to the above dilemma — to 'the problem of evil' as it arises for him. We can say that the very fact that self-valuing human beings find no teleology in the world which unfailingly favours human welfare makes them fall back upon co-operative modes of action for the purpose of survival and enjoyment. The notion that the human species is on its own is born in this way. We learn that we have to look after ourselves. Species-survival is thus ensured. The *prima facie* logical embarrassment — 'the problem of evil' — is somewhat allayed. *Precisely* because we are alone in the world, we turn to each other for help, to the extent we are able and willing to help one another. But can this 'falling back upon one another' make human beings — in so far as they are non-theists — change their (apparently shocking) morally neutral attitude to unredeemable human (not to mention animal) suffering? I believe this can, and ought to, happen. But there is another important matter which we should consider before we examine this possibility in detail. This is the matter of morality. The human situation — as seen by non-theists — must lead to an increasingly co-operative style of human life. But co-operative activity need not always be of the morally commendatory sort. The life-style of hierarchical societies can be described as a co-operative life-style, but not, surely, as a morally commendatory life-style. What is morality, anyway, and what are its foundations?

II

I have argued that every human being, in so far as he is self-conscious, necessarily values himself in some sense or other. But what is this 'some sense or other'? The sense in question has to be got out of the fact that, in so far as I think the complex thought symbolised by the expression 'I', I necessarily posit myself as the object of an act of addressing, i.e. as the object of a minimally caring attitude. Now this act of positing myself as the object of care is the most fundamental mode of my being a self-conscious creature. Therefore, the minimal self-valuation which is implicit in the above act must be self-valuation in an unconditional sense, and not in the sense in which I might value myself because of what might be called my *accidental* properties — e.g. my intelligence, social usefulness, etc. Now it must be clear to me that every self-conscious human being must minimally value himself unconditionally — i.e. in the way in which I value myself. And unconditional minimal self-valuation admits of no degrees. (The kind of valuation I have in mind is ethical in character because it is *unconditional* valuation.) It would follow from this that I could never really *convince* another person that he is intrinsically less valuable than myself. I think this is the beginning of moral wisdom. This wisdom is embodied in the religious conviction that all men are equally valuable in the eyes of God.

III

An unconditionally — and logically necessarily unconditionally — minimally self-valuing creature must necessarily regard as 'unacceptable' those actions, attitudes, etc., of others which do not spring from the belief or the assumption that he is an unconditionally minimally valuable creature; and he must find 'acceptable' those actions, attitudes, etc., of others which do spring from this assumption. (It does not follow from this that it must be entirely clear to the creature what constitutes behaviour which springs from the assumption that he is an unconditionally minimally valuable creature, although he must, of course, have *some* notion of what such behaviour must be like.) Suppose a self-conscious human being, e.g. myself, tried to deny this by saying the following: 'There is no reason why others ought to behave towards me as though I were an unconditionally minimally valuable creature, because, although I cannot help regarding myself as being unconditionnally minimally valuable, I may well not be so.' Can I really think this thought? I do not think so. Because thinking this thought involves thinking the thought symbolised by the expression 'I' — i.e. it involves unconditional minimal self-valuation, and the following resultant thought would be self-discrepant: 'I am unconditionally minimally valuable, but I may well not be.' What I am driving at is this: I cannot *both* believe that I am unconditionally minimally valuable — and logically necessarily believe this — *and* fail to believe that others should behave towards me as though I *were* unconditionally valuable. Thus every self-conscious human being is committed to believing that others ought to behave towards him as though he were an unconditionally minimally valuable creature.

IV

I must also realise that every other self-conscious human being would also be committed to believing that others

should behave towards him as though he were an unconditionally minimally valuable creature. Can I, however, say
the following: 'He ought not to believe that others should
behave towards him as though he were unconditionally
minimally valuable'? This would amount to saying 'He
ought not to regard himself as being unconditionally
minimally valuable'. No human being can fail to regard
himself as being unconditionally minimally valuable, so I
cannot say of any particular person that he ought not to
regard himself as being unconditionally minimally valuable. So the situation so far is as follows: we are all
committed to believing that others ought to behave
towards us as though we were unconditionally minimally
valuable.

V

Is there any argument which would show that we are all
committed to believing that *we* ought to behave towards
others as though they were unconditionally minimally
valuable? The availability of such an argument would
depend on whether or not it is the case that I cannot —
logically cannot — help regarding others also, and not only
myself, as being valuable in some sense or other. I think it
can be shown that this is in fact the case. I think the
following utterance, say issued by me to you, is self-
discrepant: 'You are not valuable in *any* sense whatever.'
This is because in issuing this utterance to you I necessarily
address you, cast you as an object of minimal concern, i.e.
regard you, however implicitly, as being valuable in some
sense or other, so that my statement becomes self-
stultifying. But what about the following statement? '*He* is
not valuable in any sense whatever.' Is this statement
self-stultifying? The following argument, I believe, shows
that it is self-stultifying: in thinking of a 'third' person I
have to posit him as a personal subject, otherwise I would
not be able to attribute personal properties to him. Now
positing somebody — or something — as a personal subject

is inseparable from imagining that he is the object of an act of addressing. Only as involved in an act of addressing, actually or imaginatively, is it possible to think of someone as a subject. So when I think of a 'third' person, known or unknown to me, I posit him as a personal subject, i.e. I imagine him — logically necessarily imagine him — as being the object of an imagined act of addressing: i.e. as the object of a minimally caring attitude. Thus I must logically necessarily regard myself, you, and all other human beings as being objects of a minimally caring attitude — and in that sense as being necessarily 'valuable': i.e. as unconditionally deserving of a minimally caring attitude. If I could regard you, him, and others, as not being valuable at all, it should be possible for me to think of you, him, and others, *without* casting you, him and others, as objects of minimal concern. And this I cannot do. We are talking here of logical commitment, not of what people actually say they believe. It would follow from this that I am committed to believing — a fact which I may of course self-deceivingly conceal from myself — that I ought to behave towards everyone as I would expect them to behave towards me — i.e. as beings who unconditionally deserve minimal care.

VI

I had said earlier (section I) that it should be possible for the non-theist to abandon his apparently shocking attitude of moral neutrality towards humanly unredeemable human (not to mention animal) suffering. In the light of the above discussion of the foundations of morality I can now attempt to indicate how the non-theist may do this.

I have argued that we all — in so far as we are un-selfdeceivingly self-conscious — regard one another as unconditionally minimally valuable. Our implicit recognition of one another as being unconditionally minimally valuable is sufficient to enable us to accept a minimum stock of moral imperatives about how we should behave towards one another. I shall not attempt to specify

the nature of these imperatives here. Instead I should like
to raise the following question: Is the nature of our moral
obligation towards others such that it only enjoins us to
behave in a certain way towards others? Doesn't the nature
of our moral obligation towards others generate imperatives about what we should *wish* for them? It seems to
me that given the human condition as it is, situations
always arise where we are not able to do what we believe
we ought to do towards others, and yet our moral
obligation towards others does not come to an end in such
situations. We remain under a moral obligation to *wish*
others well, even when we are not in a position to do
anything towards their well-being.

Consider now the following situation. A man is in great
pain, despite the best and most caring medical attention. I
can *do* nothing to alleviate his pain. Clearly I am under a
moral obligation to *hope*, or where hoping is irrational, to
at least wish that his pain would lessen or disappear. But
the situation is morally non-neutral not merely in this
ordinary sense. The man is suffering beyond endurance —
it is obvious that nature is not exhibiting minimal care
towards him. The very same nature which makes it
logically necessary for me to regard him as minimally
valuable, in so far as I think of him at all. I am obliged to
see him as situated in the world — and not at all minimally
cared for. I am also obliged — in so far as I must think of
him as a personal subject — to imaginatively see him as the
object of a minimally caring communicative attention. But
how can I see him both as, and as not, minimally cared
for? Isn't this an apparent irrationality in the very nature
of things? How do I overcome this irrationality? I cannot
deceive myself into thinking that he is not really suffering
beyond endurance (although in the history of religious
thought theories have been put forward which have rested
on an attempt to deceive oneself in this way). Nor can I
not see him imaginatively as the object of minimal
concern. I may try to drift away from thinking of him
altogether — but not without self-deception. Or I may
despairingly simply *forget* him. But such forgetting would

not resolve the irrationality of the situation we are considering. (Incidentally, the irrationality exists sharply for the suffering man too. He too necessarily regards himself as being minimally valuable and finds himself forsaken. He may lapse into unconsciousness or go out of his mind — but the irrationality remains.)

What do I do then? How do *I* exhibit minimal concern for him? Clearly, I would first of all wish and hope that his suffering would not fracture his self-consciousness in such a way that it would be impossible, apparently, for me to actually or imaginatively cast him as the object of my, or anybody else's, act of addressing. For then it would appear that I would not be able at all to see him as an object of minimal concern. But suppose his suffering really is so unbearable that he is liable to suffer a breakdown of self-consciousness. What can I, ought I to, do then? I can wish him reversible unconsciousness — a sort of sleep from which, I hope, he would emerge again in this world as a self-conscious creature who is *not* suffering beyond endurance. But what if his emergence in this favourable condition is ruled out by competent medical judgement? Would I then be under a moral obligation to wish him irreversible unconsciousness, e.g. death? But to wish him death is, apparently, to make it impossible for me or anybody to see him as an object of minimal concern. Clearly I cannot, therefore, wish him death. But how can I acquiesce in his unbearable suffering? It looks as if I am under a moral obligation both to, and not to, wish him death. How can I overcome this dilemma? I am assuming that I am under a moral obligation to try to overcome this dilemma. Because if I shirk this task, I would be abandoning my commitment to regard the suffering man as an object of care.

It seems to me that I can overcome the above dilemma only by achieving a condition of thought wherein I would neither have to wish the man death, nor have to *not* wish him death, with the proviso that I achieve this condition without abandoning my commitment to regard the man as an object of care. Can I achieve this condition? It seems to

me that I can. If I invoke an infinitely loving and powerful
and wise consciousness which either miraculously resuscitates and heals the man in this world and life, or renders
him self-conscious *beyond* death, I would be spared the
dilemma of either wishing the man death or wishing him
an insufferably painful life. In either miraculously healing
the suffering man, or in resuscitating his self-consciousness
beyond death, the infinitely loving and powerful and wise
consciousness, 'God', would cast him as the object of his
care — so the man would continue to be able to be
regarded by me as an object of care. I would regard him as
the object of God's care, thereby continuing to regard him
as being minimally valuable, i.e. as self-conscious. It is
important to see here that in all this I would have to
invoke God as a real presence — I would have to seek
communicative contact with him (act as if I were doing
this). And I would have to pray to God that the man be
healed or resuscitated in the incomprehensible (to me)
'beyond death' way. Why can't I imagine that God would
automatically take care of all this without there being any
need for me to offer a petitionary prayer? I think the
answer to this question must be this. I cannot invoke an
infinitely loving, etc., consciousness in abstraction from
making clear to myself — through the mode of petitionary
prayer — my need and wish that the suffering man be
saved. (Petitionary prayer need not be sought to be
understood as being 'efficacious'. It is a mode of *grasping*
the loving character of God, however inadequately.) I can
now state shortly the moral demand which the suffering
man (he is suffering beyond endurance and is outside the
reach of medical help), or rather his situation, imposes on
me. I am, in the situation in question, under a moral
obligation to employ the language of theistic prayer —
exploratorily, but really, and not merely fancifully. (I can
communicatively — e.g. in theistic prayer — seek a
communicative being, e.g. God, without at the same time
presuming to have established his reality. See Essay 2,
'Soul', p. 41, where I make the same point, and also p. 64;
also Essay 3, 'Hoping and Wishing'.) If I don't, then I do

not escape or overcome the dilemma of either wishing the
suffering man death or an unbearably painful continuation
of life. And in employing the language of theistic prayer, I
cannot fail to affirm the reality of God (I think this is one
version of what might be called the moral-ontological
argument). It does not follow from this that I *believe* in
the reality of God, or that I *believe* that a resuscitation of
self-consciousness beyond death is possible. Nor can I *hope*
that all this is so: belief and hope are inductive concepts —
some specification of 'grounds' for believing or hoping is
always a legitimate demand. I cannot, I believe, identify
'grounds' of any intelligible kind here. Nor can I merely
wish that there were a God. This suggests that I have found
that there isn't — as yet — a God, and this is hopelessly to
misunderstand the logic of the notion of 'God'. Perhaps I
can simply *wish* that there would be a resuscitation of
self-consciousness beyond death? But an act of wishing has
the structure of exploratory communication — see Essay 3,
'Hoping and Wishing'. *In* wishing that it would be the case
that p, I inevitably think the thought 'Let it be the case
that p!'. It would be self-discrepant to say or think 'I wish
it would be the case that p, but let it not be the case that
p!' And thinking the thought 'Let it be the case that p!'
involves exploratorily issuing the utterance 'If anybody is
willing and able to make it the case that p, let him do so!'
to the entire class of actual and possible agents in the
universe, including God. I believe that the notions of God
and the resuscitation of self-consciousness are not demonstrably self-contradictory notions, although they are
essentially obscure notions. And they are morally indispensable notions, in the sense that I am under a moral
obligation to exploratorily invoke the reality of God and
his resuscitating power.

Suppose someone raises the following objection at this
stage: 'How can you invoke God when you have no
grounds for believing in his reality?' The answer to this
question must be as follows: 'Where you have the notion
of a communicative being, whose reality you have no
'grounds' for believing in, you can *look for* him by seeking

him communicatively. And to communicatively seek a communicative being is to invoke him. If you are supposed to be lost in a forest, although I have no grounds for believing that you are there, I can look for you by shouting out for you. This involves invoking you, affirming your reality, but not *believing* in your reality. Nor, of course, *disbelieving* in your reality. So I can seek to address God and pray to him — thereby affirming his reality without presuming to have established it. And I am under a moral obligation to do this.'

I am not merely under a moral obligation to pray for the resuscitation of the dead. I am also under a moral obligation to pray that they may be set in environments (whose nature and structure must remain frustratingly obscure to our this-world-oriented minds) which would further their moral and spiritual growth. And I am not merely under a moral obligation to pray for the dead. Death is not the only instance of humanly unredeemable human suffering and loss. In our individual and social life, our biological existence, or private and public lives, there are impassable difficulties, crises, contradictions, the over-coming of which is manifestly beyond human power and wisdom and love. We are under a moral obligation to invoke God in the face of all these difficulties, and not merely in the face of death. And there is also simply a need to do so. This need is not obviously universally felt by all individuals. But if there is any soundness in my arguments that as far as others are concerned, we are under a moral obligation to employ the language of theistic prayer, then there can be no serious non-theistic in-hibitions in the way of employing such language in relation to oneself.

VII

If we are under an obligation to see the dead as resuscitated by God's vocative act, and set in an environ-ment which is appropriate to their need for growth, we can see how we may be under an obligation to kill a man without ceasing to at least minimally value him. Suppose in self-defence, or in the defence of others, I have to kill a human being — let us call him X. In killing X I make him unavailable to me, and make everybody — the living — unavailable to him (it is in this respect that the badness of solitary confinement approaches the badness of killing). And in so far as valuing somebody, however minimally, requires the general communicative availability of the person who is sought to be valued, clearly I cannot, having killed X, value him, or believe that anybody else among the living can value him. It looks as if I cannot both be under a moral obligation to kill X *and* value him, however minimally. This would be a logically fatal dilemma if the idea of God and his resuscitating power were not available to us. But it is. I can think of X as being addressed by God and as being in his care — we having failed X. How did we fail X? We lacked the power and love and opportunity to change X, make him non-injurious to others. We *had* to kill him. But this act is not incompatible with the principle of minimal valuation of persons, because we are able to, at least exploratorily-communicatively, appeal to God to rescue X from our morally handicapped situation, a situation which requires the excommunication of X from the world of the living. In so far as the picture of God's resuscitating power has a foundation in our lives, we need not despair. X is not beyond care, he is only beyond *our* capacities for caring.

It should be pointed out at once, however, that the availability of the idea of God's saving power does not give us a licence to kill. *Our* understanding of what it is to care for a person, say X, is such that killing X must be at least *prima facie* incompatible with any resolve to care for X. We must make killing as unnecessary and avoidable as we can, because our notion of caring requires the *being-together* of those who would care for one another. When we *are* constrained to kill, we invite total moral confusion and despair. We are saved, in these constraining situations, only by the idea of God's resuscitating power.

VIII

A point about the words 'Thy will be done!'. My own moral imagination, human moral imagination, is too limited and corrupted to conceive adequately what is good for the dead and the living — beyond certain limits. We must of course unceasingly exercise our moral imagination to generate visions of the good which we can realise, and to articulate petitionary and other kinds of prayer where our capacities fail us. But beyond a certain point it is quite sufficient to form the notion of God — an infinitely loving and powerful and wise consciousness — and simply invoke him and say 'Thy will be done', because by definition the fulfilment of God's will must encompass the totality of good. So I am not for the non-theist overburdening his moral imagination and trying to work out, for instance, a quite complete blueprint for what must or ought to happen for the dead, and invoking God merely as a computer. Moral humility should limit, without discouraging, the task of envisioning the good in areas where our moral capacities are unreliable. It would seem to me particularly futile and unedifying for non-theists, or even theists, to inaugurate raucous debates about the relative moral merits of reincarnation, or spirit-existence, or resurrection, and so on. 'Thy will be done!' — that should be sufficient.

IX

While on the subject of theistic prayer, I should like to give an account of idol-worship which is suggested by my general account of prayer and my analysis of the notion of 'soul'.

A sort of criticism of idol-worship, with which Hindus are often confronted, runs as follows: 'How can you worship, pray to, a piece of stone, a painting, or any other kind of image? God is not a piece of stone, a painting, or any sort of image. You are identifying God with what is manifestly *not* God'. Self-defensively, Hindus have, when confronted with the above criticism, sought to make the following reply, which, for convenience, I shall express in the first person singular: 'This statue, which you call a piece of stone, is not *in itself* the Divine Mother whom I worship. It merely *symbolises* the infinite compassion and protective power of the Divine Mother. It is a *representation*, merely, of her. My mind wanders easily. It needs a point of concentration, a focus of attention, to enable me to invoke Kali, the Divine Mother. You cannot accuse me of a crude identification of God with a piece of stone or whatever.'

I do not find this reply satisfactory. If the Kali-idol were merely a representation, merely an *aid* to contemplation, I could not *direct* my act of worship, my prayer, towards it. I could not feel the *kind* of awe and reverence that I do feel in its presence. If it were merely a representation, it would become redundant the moment it fulfilled its representational, contemplation-aiding, function. But this does not happen. With the greatest concentration I direct my prayer *towards* the idol, and not as towards a mere representation.

Does this make my Kali-worship a case of idolatry? (I will not here go into the unedifying question of whether the idea of Kali adequately embodies the idea of Divine Reality, the idea of God. I will assume that it does, or can, do so.) I believe the following argument should succeed in showing that my Kali-worship is *not* idolatrous. I direct a *communicative* attention towards the Kali-idol, not a merely perceptual or reflective attention, although I may do this as well, but *not* in offering worship to the idol, in addressing a prayer to it. Employing an argument which recurs throughout this book, I should now like to say the following. In directing my communicative attention towards the Kali-idol, I do indeed encounter the physicality of the idol. But I reach beyond this physicality and see it as embodying *Kali* herself, as embodying the 'Thou' which must be the mode of my thinking of Kali communicatively, non-predicatively. Not that Kali is conceived by me non-predicatively. Indeed, I attribute infinite compassion and protective power to her. But in thinking of her communicatively I reach beyond even these attributes and see her as a pure 'Thou'. In so seeing her, I do *not* think of her *referentially* as the idol confronting me. My communicative attention is directed towards the idol non-referentially. This is quite completely analogous to the way in which my communicative attention, when it is directed towards you, is also directed non-referentially towards you. *In* seeing you as a soul, I do not think of you as, for example, the young man standing in front of me. If, on being plainly addressed by me, you were to ask, 'Who do you mean?' (of course you would allow yourself the right to ask this question only as a piece of philosophical eccentricity) and I were to say, 'The young man standing in front of me', you would or should be profoundly puzzled. You could ask me, 'Who do you mean by the young man standing in front of me?' And I could only reply 'You', thereby vocatively, and non-referentially, *meaning* you. Of course you would have to be a certain sort of being in order for me to be able to vocatively *mean* you. But for all that, *in* vocatively meaning you, I do not mean 'a certain sort of being'.

But how does all this apply to my worship of Kali? In the following way. *In* vocatively *meaning* her, in seeing her as a 'Thou', I do not mean 'the statue in front of me'. So I do not, categorically do not, identify her – the 'Thou' I invoke in addressing her – with the, if you like, piece of stone towards which I direct my communicative attention. But what is the role of the statue then? It is a religious work of art, sanctioned by tradition, which symbolises Kali's divine attributes. (It could also be a piece of abstract art, sanctioned by contemporary aesthetic sensibility.) But the statue does not symbolise Kali as a representation whose original is *somewhere else*. I conceive of Kali as an omnipresent caring power. The statue symbolises these attributes of her and holds them together in one place, i.e. in the body of the statue itself. In this way the statue symbolises Kali's omnipresence and invites attention to this fact by the very specificity of its body and its place (if she is everywhere then she is where the statue is, *in* the statue, as well). And it is in acknowledgement of her omnipresence that I direct my communicative attention towards the statue. (My notion of her omnipresence would be quite bogus if I was unable quite specifically to direct my attention to the body and place of the statue. 'She is everywhere, but how can she be *here*?' — this would be a subtly self-discrepant thought.)

It would be the worst sort of physicalist ridiculousness to think that a chemical examination of the statue would reveal the 'Thou' I see Kali as in communicatively attending to the statue. Certainly as ridiculous as supposing that a chemical examination of your body would reveal the soul, the 'you', I see you as in communicatively identifying you. (In seeing you communicatively I associate with you a kind of 'magnetism' which is as indubitable as it is physicalistically unintelligible. In seeing the statue of Kali communicatively, I would similarly be enabled to imagine a 'halo' around it — the halo of communicative availability.)

Suppose someone were to say the following now: 'Even if your arguments so far are sound, addressing Kali is possible only if you *believe* in the reality of Kali. Do you?' Now if I believed in the reality of Kali, my idol-worship of her would be a quite straightforward mode of worshipping her, praying to her. I might of course still need the kinds of argument that I have been trying to develop above to rid myself of the fear of idolatry. But suppose I have no grounds for believing or disbelieving in the reality of Kali, suppose I merely have the conviction that the idea of an omnipresent, etc., caring power is not a demonstrably self-contradictory idea. Given this, can't I exploratorily-communicatively seek Kali by the exploratorily-communicatively directing my communicative attention towards her statue? I believe I can; let me explain how.

Consider the following chain of thoughts: 'If Kali is real, she must be everywhere, including that statue. And she must be communicatively available — how can she be caring if she is not? I can direct the following thought towards the idol: "If you are there, I want to confess to you, thank you, seek your help." But I don't say or think, "If you are not there, don't bother!" That would be absurd. Who would I be saying that to? But perhaps I can think this: "Kali is not real, then my would-be, exploratory, communicative thoughts and words in relation to her are empty agitations of the mind." But I don't *know* that Kali is unreal. So I cannot but see the force of my would-be exploratory-communicative thoughts and words in relation to her as being indistinguishable from the force of such thoughts and words accompanied by *belief* in the reality of Kali. For even in thinking a would-be communicative thought in relation to her, I have to invoke her as a presence. So although the force of my communicative thoughts and words in relation to her must remain exploratory in character, I can quite straightforwardly employ the standard language of Kali-invocation, for I do really invoke her. Of course I needn't always invoke her in relation to her idol, I can "pray in my heart" to her. But no philosophical inhibitions need prevent me from participating in Kali-invocation, or from solitarily engaging in such invocation, where the focus of attention is an idol. And such invocation does not amount to idolatry.'

If the above chain of thoughts embodies sound reasoning, and I believe it does, then a very wide area of religious life becomes available to those who are unable to accept cognitivist theism.

X

I had argued that the non-theist, especially an evolutionary non-theist who also — as I think he must — believes in the coherence of reality, faces a 'problem of evil' of a special kind. He finds that the very nature of self-consciousness — a product of evolution — logically obliges him to regard all human beings as being minimally valuable. And yet at the same time he is constrained to recognise that the very same nature out of which self-consciousness has evolved is very far indeed from being — all too often — even minimally hospitable to human beings. He detects an apparent contradiction at the very heart of the nature of things, in the way in which the theist finds the relationship between an all-powerful and loving God and suffering humanity logically and morally embarrassing. Now if my arguments have been sound, the non-theist's problem of evil poses a moral challenge to him which leads — or ought to lead — him to acknowledge the necessity — the moral necessity — of non-cognitivistically, and yet unambiguously, employing the language of theistic prayer. But in so far as there remains the theistic problem of evil, there must be at the heart of theistic consciousness a profound agony and despair. The non-theist must share with the theist this agony and despair. And clarifications of the theistic problem of evil must deeply enrich the non-theist's moral imagination.

5 The Mystical

I

'There are, indeed, things that cannot be put into words' – so says Wittgenstein in the *Tractatus* (6.522). One could say that belief in the truth of this statement of Wittgenstein's constitutes the essential minimum condition which must be fulfilled if one is to at all sympathetically approach the notion of 'the mystical'. Wittgenstein is not saying that there are things (e.g. complex states of mind, attitudes, relationships, etc.) which are *very hard*, impossible for all except the exceptionally linguistically gifted, to describe. He is saying, surely, that it is logically impossible to put certain things into words, or impossible in some other fundamental sense. Can we believe this? What would it be like to *try* to believe this statement? Surely we cannot, in the ordinary way, try to think of *examples* of things or kinds of things about which we cannot – logically cannot – say anything (i.e. anything significant). For it would appear that to 'think of anything' at all would be to bring that thing under some description or other, and so that thing would no longer be strictly indescribable. Suppose, however, that I tried to think of something which might be called 'the universe' or 'reality as a whole' or 'the totality or system of all actual and possible states of affairs', or something like that. Now it is clear that in so far as I succeed in thinking of such a thing, let us call it R, I would not be bringing R under any description at all. R would be inclusive of whatever description I might want to bring R under, otherwise it would not be R. For any particular description of R would be the description of some state of affairs or other of which R must — if it is the totality or system of all actual and possible states of affairs — already be inclusive. Thus R would be indescribable — logically so. But could it be that 'R' expresses a self-contradictory thought? Wittgenstein says, 'The totality of existing states of affairs is the world' (*Tractatus*, 2.04). Surely he should have said 'The totality or system of existing and possible states of affairs is the world'. This is because the notion of 'the world' must be the notion of that which is inclusive also of the realm of possibility, and not merely the realm of actuality. Un-realised possibilities contribute as much to the character of the world as realised possibilities. Anyway, I think we could say that Wittgenstein would not have regarded 'R' as expressing a self-contradictory thought. But there is really no need to appeal to the authority of Wittgenstein to see that 'R' cannot be regarded as expressing a self-contradictory thought. What gives significance to any factual proposition is a particular state of affairs, actual or possible, which it successfully represents: or rather, the *nexus* of the state of affairs, actual or possible, represented by the proposition and the state of affairs *excluded* by it. But the notion of any such particular nexus has significance because, among other things, we are able to contrast it with the idea of the nexus which is the *totality* or system of actual and possible states of affairs, i.e. with the thought we try to represent by 'R'. Now what contributes to the significance of the notion of a particular nexus of actual and possible state of affairs cannot be self-contradictory. So the thought we seek to express by 'R' cannot be self-contradictory. But it does not follow from this that this thought is comprehensible. I take it to be a necessary condition of something being comprehensible that it should, in principle, be describable. But the object of the thought we seek to express by 'R' is not even *in principle* describable. And yet reference to this thought is unavoidably linked up with the acknowledgement of the significance of any proposition — any factual proposition. So all factual discourse presupposes the notion of something which is incomprehensible. Why cannot we call this notion *a* notion of the mystical?

II

Consider the proposition: 'Something exists.' Nothing can be more apparently ordinary than what is asserted by this proposition. But consider the proposition which is its contradictory, the proposition 'Nothing exists.' This proposition defies understanding because the concept of absolute nothingness which it employs defies understanding. We cannot *imagine* absolute nothingness, we can form no clear thought about it. And yet the perfectly simple, even banal, proposition 'something exists' makes necessary reference to the proposition 'Nothing exists'. One can again say that the former proposition makes necessary reference to another notion of the mystical. Heidegger's question, 'Why is there something, and not rather nothing?', should not be taken literally, because we cannot grasp the notion of absolute nothingness. His question should be treated as an invitation to us to contemplate the implicatedness of the proposition 'something exists' in the notion — *a* notion — of the mystical, i.e. a notion of something about which nothing clear can be said, but which is nevertheless indispensable. However, it is precisely the unintelligibility of the notion of absolute nothingness which makes it possible for us not to slip into a doctrine of 'mysticism' with regard to it. (Is the phrase 'absolute nothingness' a nonsense-phrase? I don't think so. We are constrained to acknowledge its significance when we try to grasp the *mode of being* of non-subjective being, i.e. matter, or when we contemplate the possibility of personality-annihilation at death.) Doctrines of mysticism should be distinguished from the necessity of acknowledging dimensions of the indescribable, the essentially unclear, etc., which may harmlessly — but *not* trivially — be called the necessity of acknowledging dimensions of the mystical.

Somebody may argue that the fact that the proposition

'nothing exists' is essentially unintelligible should make us want to suspect the intelligibility of the proposition 'something exists'. But this would be pure dogma. In fact it is a dogma of logical theory that the intelligibility, meaningfulness, comprehensibility, etc., of a proposition entails the intelligibility, meaningfulness, comprehensibility, etc., of the contradictory of the given proposition. And conversely, that the unintelligibility of a proposition entails the unintelligibility of the proposition which constitutes its logical contradiction. Rejection of this dogma is the basis of my attempt here to introduce the notion of the mystical into our conceptual framework without being committed to any doctrines of mysticism.

It might also be urged that the notion of an unintelligible proposition is not a viable notion. But then the choice would be between accepting the viability of the notion of an unintelligible, incomprehensible, etc. proposition and the view that some significant propositions do not have contradictories. The second alternative would destroy logical theory. Acceptance of the first alternative only involves the rejection of a *dogma* of logical theory.

Is the proposition 'something exists' *really* an unintelligible proposition? It is clearly the presupposition of every affirmative existential proposition. That there are things, objects, actualities, is the clear deliverance of our consciousness, which is always consciousness *of* something or other.

I must confess to a feeling of dissatisfaction with the way I have thus far presented the argument of this section. Let me try another strategy. I think it would be conceded, even by those who are sceptical about the legitimacy of the proposition 'something exists', that in acknowledging the existence of anything whatever, one implicitly thinks, or tries to think, the thought expressible by the words 'something, as opposed to nothing, exists'. Now this thought, reference to which is necessarily made in acknowledging the existence of anything whatever, is essentially incomprehensible, because it employs the notion of absolute nothingness — which is an incomprehensible notion. This is another way of saying that all existential discourse is logically tied up with an incomprehensible notion — the notion of absolute nothingness. I would like to say that this amounts to the same thing as saying that all existential discourse makes reference to a notion of the mystical.

III

One is inclined to think that the thoughts expressed by the words 'I exist' or 'I am conscious' are deeply implicated in some dimension or other of the mystical. I am inclined to doubt this. This is because the denials of what is expressed by these thoughts are straightforward self-contradictions. There is inevitably associated with the thoughts 'I exist' or 'I am conscious' a bewildering sense of triviality. We might pompously say that this is existential, and not merely logical, triviality, but both kinds of triviality have to do with the fact that the contradictories of certain thoughts are self-contradictions. Of course one can *worry* about existential triviality — the absurdity of the utterly un-problematic character of our distinctive mode of being, which is the conscious or self-conscious mode of being. But this worry is not to be identified with the mystical preoccupation with the notion of self-consciousness. Para-doxically, one can say that the mystery of self-consciousness consists in its utterly unmysterious (existentially trivial) character.

It is quite different, however, with the thought ex-pressed by the words 'I am alive'. Do these words express a significant thought? I think so, despite the great difficulty — if not impossibility — of explicating the notion of one's own death, a notion which is clearly implicated with the notion of one's being alive, which figures in the thought 'I am alive'. Minimally, this thought expresses my knowledge that I am *not* dead, that there does not exist in the world a corpse which can, in principle, be identified by others as *my corpse*. The thought, and the knowledge it expresses, are not trivial. One can easily imagine circumstances where one's *utterance* 'I am alive' would be entirely apposite, e.g., when one has mistakenly been taken for dead. Consider, however, the contradictory of the thought 'I am alive', i.e. the thought 'I am not alive' or 'I am dead'. Now this thought, unlike the thoughts 'I am not conscious' or 'I do not exist', is not a piece of self-contradiction — another reason why the thought 'I am alive' is not a trivial thought. The thought 'I am not alive' at once plunges one into the essential unclearness and incomprehensibility of the notion of disembodied existence. For I could think the thought 'I am not alive' only if I had, as it were, lost my body. (I take the thought 'I am not alive' as equivalent to the thought 'I am not corporeal at all'. I do not take it as equivalent to the thought 'I have *no* animation'. Presumably, in order to think the thought 'I am not alive' I would have to be in some sense non-corporeally animated. But is the notion of non-corporeal animation a comprehensible notion? I don't think so, although it is not a demonstrably self-discrepant notion.) So here we have another example of a perfectly comprehensible thought — i.e. the thought 'I am alive' — whose contradictory is *not* comprehensible, yet reference to which is, by reason of logic, unavoidable if one is to think the thought 'I am alive'. Here is another notion of the mystical. Another, an orthodox way of making this point would be this: what is mystical is not the mere fact of my being a conscious or a self-conscious being, but the fact that I am an incarnate consciousness. Perhaps by (I think mistakenly) seeing the fact of self-consciousness itself as *a (the)* profound mystery, various philosophies of mysticism have gone astray — missed the authentic involvement of the notion of an incarnate consciousness in the mystical dimension.

Consider now the thought expressed by the words 'We are alive'. Clearly this thought is a significant and comprehensible thought. It is a thought which is intimately shared by all 'survivors' — by all those who, in a context of mutual awareness, are witness to the death of another or of others. 'We are alive' minimally expresses the knowledge that we are not yet corpses. However, the contradictory of the thought 'We are alive', i.e., the thought 'We are *not* alive', is an utterly unclear thought, although not a self-contradictory thought; it embodies the idea — hopelessly enmeshed in the mystical dimension — of a communal disembodied existence, of communication between disembodied selves.

IV

In an earlier section I had argued that every affirmative existential judgement referred indirectly to the essentially incomprehensible notion of absolute nothingness, and was in this way tied up with a notion of the mystical. My argument was that it is the presupposition of any affirmative existential judgement, e.g. that X exists, that something, as opposed to nothing, existed; and that this presupposition involved the employment of the mystical notion of absolute nothingness. Consider now the following, slight variation, of this argument.

We not only affirm the existence of things, we also notice the occurrence of events. We think thoughts of the form 'X has occurred' or 'X is occurring' or 'X occurred', where 'X' is the name of some event. Now I think it must be the presupposition of thoughts of these sorts that something, as opposed to nothing, has occurred, is occurring, occurred, etc. And this presupposition involves the employment of the notion of *nothing* occurring. This is the essentially incomprehensible notion of 'time standing still', or the notion of timelessness or eternity. Another mystical notion at the heart of a perfectly ordinary mode of thinking.

V

The notion of a 'mystical state' or 'mystical state of consciousness' are central to mystic teaching. One question one is inclined to ask in this connection is: 'What is a *non-mystical* state of consciousness?' The following is an attempt to arrive at some sort of answer to this, I think fundamental, question in the philosophy of mysticism.

Philosophical questions arise, or can be raised, in a variety of situations: in actual or anticipated conversation, discussion, dialogue, etc., between two or more persons; in solitary meditation in a soliloquised form; in action or activity, momentous or trivial. Consider the last type of situation. On the brink of doing some action or other, an individual or a group of individuals can ask the moral question: ought I (we) to do this thing? If this question is a genuinely moral question, then it is also, at least, a philosophical question, i.e. it would belong to the family of questions about the nature and interrelationship of concepts which is — obstinate scepticism apart — readily identifiable as the substance of philosophical inquiry. (I think this fact throws light on the frustratingly imperfect resolution of most moral problems — the underlying conceptual confusions are never adequately sorted out, whether one perceives this or not.) I would say that the situations in which moral questions arise are more or less 'momentous' situations. These situations form a class apart from the vast majority of situations which do not generate the kind of urgency and sense of responsibility characteristic of moral questioning. But these, non-momentous, situations can also give rise to philosophical questioning. Suddenly, some quite trivial act or activity or state of mind or mode of being may pose a fundamental question about the very meaning of things, the very nature of what it is for anything at all to be there. The mode of questioning here would be characterised by a sense of absurdity, dizziness (as Wittgenstein uses this word), even hopelessness. But in so far as one brings one's conceptual intelligence to bear upon the questions that arise here, these questions would quickly take the shape of philosophical questions. (Why does a sense of despair characterise the asking of a genuine moral question of the form 'What ought I to do?'. Not only because an answer may be urgently needed, but because of the kind of question to which an answer is here sought in a hurry. Philosophical questions cannot be answered in a hurry. A criss-cross, synoptic investigation, or family of investigations, is required for the solution or understanding of philosophical questions.)

Let us take a closer look at the context of philosophical *discussion*. It is not just a psychological prerequisite but a logical requirement that philosophical discussion be conducted in an unhurried and open-ended manner. The observance of this requirement entails that participants in philosophical discussion deliberately introduce an *element* of, or, better, an *attitude* of what I would like to call *timelessness* into their conversational situation. (It may be, probably is the case, that this is a requirement of other kinds of discussion as well, e.g. religious or literary discussions – I am not sure.) But this modification of their ordinary conversational situation must be deliberate in the sense that the fact that it *is* a modification of their conversational situation is not lost sight of by the participants.(There are two reasons why I am labouring this point: (i) I think it has an interest of its own, which I have not, however, spelt out at all adequately; (ii) I think it is sufficient to show that consciousness of being engaged in philosophical inquiry cannot be coexistensive with consciousness of being in a communicative situation. It can only be a modification, and, therefore, a detail of the latter.)

There is an important consequence of this. This is that all philosophical discussion, *notwithstanding* its extraordinary importance (the inculcation of an attitude of timelessness with regard to it would confer this importance on it), presupposes the massive clarity of the ordinary conversational situation. Further consequences of this are: first, that whatever clarity is reached in philosophical discussion, this clarity cannot exceed the clarity of the ordinary conversational situation which is a presupposition of the conduct of any philosophical discussion; second, that the conversational situation cannot *itself* be brought into question in philosophical discussion — to try to do so would be to pretend to be unclear about that, clarity regarding which is a presupposition of any philosophical discussion. Thus in any philosophical discussion, a search for what is really *given* for human thought and reflection must be a pseudo-search: because the givenness of the conversational situation is the presupposition of all philo-sophical discussion. Nothing, in philosophical discussion, can be found to be given in a more basic sense than the conversational situation itself. Third, philosophical dis-cussion — the whole mode of raising and trying to answer philosophical questions — must be seen as a *feature of*, a *detail* of, the conversational mode of human life. This is what makes it possible both to commence and to discontinue philosophical discussion.

But what if philosophical questions arise and are raised in solitary meditation — in a soliloquised form? Now it seems to me that soliloquy can only be satisfactorily interpreted as a mode of operation of the imagination — a mode of operation of the imagination which consists in the solitary thinker *imagining* that he is in communicative contact with another person, i.e. in the solitary thinker imaginatively placing himself in a conversational (ordinary conversational) situation. The clarity of any piece of soliloquising cannot exceed the clarity of the imagined conversational situation which is the presupposition of soliloquising. So whether philosophical questions are sought to be answered in discussion, or in soliloquy, the whole enterprise of philosophical investigation presupposes the massive clarity of the ordinary conversational situation, and must be seen as a peculiarly intense feature or detail of it. Perhaps Wittgenstein had something like this in mind when he wrote:

> The real discovery is the one that makes me capable of stopping doing philosophy when I want to. — The one that gives philosophy peace, so that it is no longer tormented by questions which bring *itself* in question. Instead, we now demonstrate a method, by examples, and the series of examples can be broken off. — Problems are solved (difficulties eliminated), not a *single* problem. (*Philosophical Investigations, 133*)

Now what I have called the clarity of the ordinary conversational situation is something regarding which nothing can be said which would be a paradigm of clarity in human thinking, because whatever is sought to be said or thought about it would have to be said or thought in discussion or soliloquy, and would, for that reason, presuppose the clarity of the ordinary conversational situation. Of course, this clarity *makes itself manifest* whenever we are in communicative contact with another person or whenever we *think*. (The clarity of self-consciousness is merely an imaginative mode of the clarity of the communicative situation.) Here is another area of the mystical — a *clarity* and not a piece of *obscurity*, about which nothing can be said in clarification, but which makes itself manifest.

It is not easy psychologically to accept the view that philosophical inquiry can only take place *within* the matrix of the ordinary conversational situation and cannot yield clarity which exceeds the clarity of this situation. Because the ordinary conversational situation is regarded as mundane, too ordinary and everyday, and surely philosophy must seek after and attain a greater clarity and perspicuousness! But this is a thoroughly muddled attitude. As I have tried to show, the ordinary conversational situation and the clarity which characterises it adequately meet our expectation that something mystical must be the foundation of all our inquiries into the nature of things. Suppose, however, that this clarity is rejected by a thinker who aspires after a greater clarity. Two options are closed to him. He cannot engage in any discussion with others in order to find this clarity, for all discussion presupposes the foundational clarity of the ordinary conversational situation. Nor can he engage in solitary meditation which consists in *thinking*, soliloquising, for that too, as I tried to show earlier, would be an exercise founded upon the clarity of the ordinary conversational situation. The only option open to our thinker is somehow to try to bypass all situations where the clarity of the ordinary conversational situation is a necessary presupposition of inquiry and where this clarity is unexceedable. He can quite easily opt out of philosophical discussions. (Can it not be that the sense of the futility of philosophical discussion, which is so important an element in the mystic's make-up, springs from his unacknowledged realisation that the clarity of the ordinary conversational situation is unexceedable?) But he must also, if this is possible, opt out of the situation of soliloquising. He can do this only by bringing about a fundamental transformation of the nature of self-consciousness. He must 'stop thinking' (witness mystical injunctions about quietening the mind, etc.). He must lose all sense of 'I', for to think the thought symbolised by the expression 'I' is, it seems to me, to posit, imaginatively, a communicative situation involving oneself and an imagined 'other' person. All the postures of classical mysticism are necessary consequences of this attempt to bypass soliloquy. I used the word 'postures' just now. But I could have instead spoken of 'experience'. Mystical experiences are, I suspect, like dream-experiences in the following respect: they are experiences which people suffer under the handicap of a more or less temporary, but total, loss of capacity for soliloquising. Thus *while* the mystical experience is being undergone the mystic can say or think nothing about it. And, of course, when the mystical experience has faded out, the mystic would not want to say anything about it. For to do so would be to make the clarity — alleged clarity — of the mystical experience subservient to the clarity of the ordinary conversational situation, to bypass which was the whole object of the exercise in consciousness-transformation. These remarks about mystic experience are not intended to be perjorative, only clarificatory of one aspect of the large topic of mystic experience.

It might be argued that the conversational situation which I imagine in soliloquy — indeed, in order to be able to soliloquise — is not what I have called the 'ordinary' conversational situation. It might be urged that the imagined hearer or speaker in soliloquy is not spatiotemporally located, unlike speakers and hearers in ordinary face-to-face conversational situations. I think this is a valid point but it does not destroy my argument. There are conversational situations — e.g. communication through correspondence — where neither party may be in a position to spatiotemporally locate the other; and yet such conversational situations would be characterised by a certain fundamental clarity, although not by the *most* fundamental clarity which can only characterise face-to-face conversational situations. But the clarity of the latter, foundational type of conversational situation (and it is also the 'ordinary' sort of conversational situation) would be presupposed by the former, impoverished, type of conversational situation. So even in soliloquy, the clarity of the ordinary conversational situation is (although it enters the situation indirectly or parasitically) the fundamental presupposition of all other sorts of clarity.

VI

A central conviction of Wittgenstein's in the *Philosophical Investigations* is that what is *given* are forms of life. Now at the heart of the cluster of forms of life which are distinctively human is the ordinary conversational form of life. The ordinary conversational situation then is what is *given* in the most fundamental sense of that word. But it is not what is *given* in the sense that what is truly 'there' can be *constructed* out of it in some way, treating it as some sort of 'datum'. The clarity of the ordinary conversational situation is unexceedable, and it makes itself manifest. Nothing can be said about it which would be clearer than its manifestation. It is what is truly 'there' in and for human life. The questions 'What is given?' and 'What is there?' coincide here. I began this section by wondering what a *non-mystical* consciousness would be like. The ordinary conversational situation is characterised by mutuality, reciprocity, etc. This consciousness, or rather the clarity of this consciousness, is the paradigm and presupposition of all other forms of consciousness, including what is called mystical consciousness. But is this given consciousness non-mystical? Well, it makes itself manifest and its clarity is unexceedable by any statement that we might make about it. In this sense nothing can — need — be said about it. Does not all this fulfil our craving for the mystical?

6 The Miraculous

I

I shall introduce the notion of the miraculous by recapitulating an argument I employed in the preceding essay about the notion of absolute nothingness. I argued that there can be nothing more uncontroversially intelligible and true than the proposition 'something exists'. And yet consider the contradictory of this proposition, the proposition 'Nothing exists'. Is this a self-contradictory proposition? I do not think so, because I do not think the proposition 'something exists' is trivially true. The thought it embodies is the clear cognitive deliverance of our consciousness, which is consciousness of something or other. But it can hardly be maintained that the proposition 'nothing exists' is a comprehensible proposition, because it can hardly be maintained that the notion of absolute nothingness which it presupposes is a comprehensible notion — although it is not a demonstrably self-contradictory notion. The notion of absolute nothingness is deeply implicated in every affirmative existential judgement, although itself an incomprehensible notion. The thoughts, 'The notion of absolute nothingness is not a demonstrably self-discrepant notion' and 'Something exists', together generate the idea of the miraculous — the idea of something coming out of nothing. It is in this sense that I shall be operating with the notion of the miraculous in this essay.

I shall not, in this essay, try to construe the miraculous as involving a suspension of the laws of nature. And not only because of the unclearness of the idea of a suspension of the laws of nature, nor even because the employment of this idea to understand the miraculous would jettison any attempt to understand the religious idea of *nature* itself being miraculously created by God out of nothing. I reject the attempt to understand the miraculous in terms of the idea of a suspension of the laws of nature on the ground that such an idea ties the miraculous to an anterior explanatory condition, thereby robbing it of its miraculous character. The miraculous, on such an account, becomes intelligible in the way in which anarchy in society becomes intelligible on the supposition that the laws of state and society have been temporarily suspended. But the miraculous must lack this kind of intelligibility. It must retain the purity of its unconnectedness with any anterior explanatory causality or condition. And this it can do only if it is seen as originating from nothing, so that there literally is nothing which can be an anterior explanatory condition of it. Any approach to the subject of the miraculous — e.g. probability theory — which seeks to make the miraculous *explicable* must be doomed to failure. The miraculous cannot, almost by definition, be explained. But it can be identified and sought to be understood. As I shall try to point out in the following sections, the idea of something coming out of nothing is unexplainedly, but readily, available in our ordinary life.

II

In the above section I have spoken of the notion of the miraculous as the notion of something coming out of nothing. This is not a satisfactory way of talking about the notion. Something 'coming out' of nothing is something materialising, happening, etc., as a result of some *process* or other — the kind of process which the phrase 'coming out of' suggests, 'nothingness' being as it were a sort of receptacle which pours out something or other. The purity of the notion of the miraculous can be preserved only if we disabuse ourselves of such images. If the miraculous is something which is a product of some process or other, then there cannot be any use for the mystical notion of absolute nothingness in order to understand — to the extent we can — the notion of the miraculous. There is nothing, no antecedent causal history, and then there is something — that is the structure of the miraculous, whether we are trying to think of the coming into being of the universe out of nothing, or of the coming into being *within the universe* of something from nothing. I have never understood why an alleged miracle-worker, if he *is* a miracle-worker, should go through some ritual or other in order miraculously to materialise something. The ritual becomes a process, or part of a process, and the allegedly miraculous coming into being of something is no longer describable as the coming into being of something from nothing. The happening has, apparently, an immediate causal past, and cannot be said to be miraculous.

III

Does the notion of a miracle presuppose the idea of a miracle-worker? Can we imagine something coming into being, apparently from nothing — of its own accord, as it were, off its own bat, and not as a result of it being willed and brought into existence by an agent? I do not think so. We can imagine the wildest improbabilities coming off in the universe — because there is a finite, as opposed to nil, probability of their coming off — but such happenings are at least *in principle* comprehensible within the framework of a physical theory which has no use for the notion of the miraculous. I suppose there is a finite probability, as opposed to zero probability, that the ink-pot in front of me should turn into a paper-weight as a result of some wild improbabilities of material rearrangement coming off. But were this to happen, I would not be under any pressure to describe the happening as miraculous. A wildly improbable rearrangement of material particles has taken place and a long causal story would have to be told in addition to saying this — but nothing has come into being from nothing. No miracle has taken place. But suppose I am able to believe that the impetus for material rearrangement came from some agent, i.e. that the causal story which I would tell, were I in possession of the necessary physical knowledge, would terminate in some action or other of some agent and not go on indefinitely into the past. In this case while I would not regard the turning of the ink-pot into a paper-weight as a miraculous happening, I would certainly regard the impetus-giving action which started the whole thing as miraculous. Provided that the action was a non-instrumental action.

IV

What do I mean by a non-instrumental action? I mean by the phrase 'non-instrumental action' an action which is such that its agent is unable to answer the question 'How did you do it?' or the question 'What means did you employ to do it?' (For a similar notion, see A.C. Danto, 'Basic Actions', in *Philosophy of Action*, ed. A. White.) It is clear that we are able to perform a vast variety of non-instrumental actions. Raising one's arm, bending one's finger — in normal circumstances — and mental acts like hoping, wishing, wondering, suspecting, etc., are actions which satisfy the criterion of an action being a non-instrumental action. And they satisfy another condition. In answer to the question 'How did you bend your finger?' I cannot say: 'Neurophysiological events $e_i \ldots e_n$ took place, then my finger got bent.' I am unable to specify anything in the past which is at all relevant to my experience of bending my finger — no action, nor any events. In a way I bring my act of finger-bending from nothing. My non-instrumental action is a miracle. All non-instrumental actions are miracles. But of course not all actions are non-instrumental actions. The act of fighting the Bangladesh war in 1971 involved the performance by thousands of people of thousands of non-instrumental actions, but it was not itself a non-instrumental act.

V

A necessary condition of a happening being miraculous is

that it should be miraculous to the person who brings it about. This is true of non-instrumental actions. Not only is there a great sense of wonder about how anyone is able to, e.g., bend his finger, but the person who bends his finger is equally awestruck by his performance (were he to think about it at all). The so-called miracle-worker who *knows how to* bring about a certain happening cannot regard that happening as being miraculous. His audience might. But after they are told that the performer has some secret powers (and knowledge of secret powers) which bring about the remarkable happening, they would be entitled not to regard the happening as being at all miraculous. I think it is best to regard such happenings as ununderstood natural phenomena which conceivably would be understood one day. Any sort of mumbo-jumbo followed by a remarkable happening could safely be put into this class of happenings. But the most trivial non-instrumental action is miraculous. It is not a natural phenomenon which will one day be understood in terms of physical principles or neurophysiological principles. We just are able to *do* certain things non-instrumentally, and this involves bringing about something which, in a sense, has no past which we can intelligibly connect with it. It is a case of something coming into being from nothing. It is a miracle.

It is interesting to consider what the Book of Genesis says about God creating the world. It is said there that God created the world and *saw* that it was good. He did not, as it were, *see to it* that it was good. The world was not created by him by means of instrumental actions. He just — non-instrumentally — created the world, and was as struck by its wonderfulness as any of us can be, i.e. when we are not thinking of the problem of evil.

I do not know whether God exists or not — I have not thought enough about the matter. But even the believer can have no intellectually comprehensible notion of the mode of God's agency. What sorts of non-instrumental actions does God perform? Whatever they are, they must be miraculous, because all non-instrumental actions are miraculous. This conclusion one can reach even if one has not thought adequately about God's existence. If God exists, his non-instrumental actions must be miracles. However, in view of our utter ignorance about the mode of God's agency, we should regard the various phenomena of cures and materialisations and so on as ununderstood natural phenomena or as mysteries — unfathomable by us. In any case they are not to be regarded as miracles. They may be seen by the devout as effects in the world of God's miraculous non-instrumental agency.

VI

God says or thinks or wills 'Let there be X!', and there is X. What are we to make of this classic account of God's miraculous power? Now if the coming into being of X is related to God's willing that there be X in such a way that God's act of willing is instrumentally responsible — i.e. responsible in a manipulative way — for the coming into being of X, then the coming into being of X cannot be miraculous. Only if God's act of willing that there be X and the coming into being of X are *coincidental* can the coming into being of X be miraculous, because it would simply be the name of a non-instrumental action of God's. I am not here trying to do theology. I am trying to understand a certain kind of theological talk. Now in the case of human non-instrumental doings — in normal circumstances — the act of willing to do something and the doing of that thing cannot be separated, they are one and the same act. And such acts are properly to be described as miraculous. So, if God exists, then it must not be supposed that his acts of willing have some tremendous manipulative power. His stock of non-instrumental actions vastly — infinitely — exceeds ours. He does not exert the force of his will upon a disobedient world. He simply does certain things — willing and doing them in the same inseparable way in which non-instrumental actions are willed and done. His acts may, of course, have consequences, quite remarkable consequences, in the world, but it is not these consequences, but the primordial acts of God, which are miraculous.

VII

There is another class of non-instrumental actions which deserves attention. They have to do with speech, communication. In normal circumstances, if I address you, your readiness to communicatively respond to my act of addressing you cannot be seen in isolation from my act. Here we witness the miracle of co-operation. Of course certain conditions have to be satisfied. If you are the person who is the recipient of my vocative act, you have to be minimally well-disposed towards me, paying heed to me, etc. But given all this, my act and your readiness to communicatively respond to it are one and the same action — a miraculous non-instrumental action. I believe this sort of action — inter-personal action — is the foundation of the entire co-operative mode of human life. One can, on this analogy, seek to understand God's persuasive agency in the world. God does not impose his will on us. But sometimes — it is said — he speaks to people in such a way that his speaking and the readiness of those to whom he speaks to listen to him, if not also to do as he says, are inseparable. But I am again doing theology without being qualified either by training or conviction to do so. Anyway, the point I wish to make is the general point about the non-instrumental, and therefore miraculous, basis — in normal circumstances — of basic co-operation-seeking communicative acts.

VIII

Consider another class of non-instrumental actions, actions which have to do with the origination and modification of experiences. Consider the non-instrumental act of opening your eyes. Visual experience becomes immediately available to you; and its availability is not separable from your act of opening your eyes. Similarly, touching something with your hands or fingers — a non-instrumental action — and the availability of tactile experience are not separable. Plugging your ears and modifying auditory experience, reaching out towards somebody in an act of love, or withdrawing from somebody, are further examples of the kind of non-instrumental actions we are considering. Not *what* we experience, but *that* we are able to experience anything at all, is miraculous. No neurophysiological theory of vision is going to compel me to ascribe a causal past to my non-instrumental act of opening my eyes and *in the same act* obtaining visual experience. I am not denying that one's eyes may get opened in other ways, and in those cases causal knowledge would of course be directly relevant. I was assuming that one can talk about a normal state of affairs in this area, a state of affairs which consists in human beings being free to open or shut their eyes, touch things with their hands or refrain from doing so, etc.

IX

I have linked the notion of the miraculous with the notion of agency, with the notion of non-instrumental agency. No metaphysical or physical theory about the world can explain how agency has come to exist in the world. Being agents ourselves we cannot step outside ourselves intellectually and see how agency has evolved out of other kinds of reality in the world. For every such act of trying to grasp the origin of agency would involve the exercise of agency — e.g. intellectual agency, thinking. How has it come about that there are creatures who are able to think? Ask questions, such as the one above? And this is also a question. That there is agency in the world is a mystery — not a mystery which, like a murder mystery, can be unravelled; but something which must for ever remain baffling to us. Men are prisoners of their sense of distinctiveness. They may well be late products of evolutionary history, but they cannot, in their innermost thoughts, believe that they are only this. Perhaps this incapacity to fully believe, contrary to available evidence, is an asset for individual as well as co-operative self-development; an asset which evolutionary history has endowed us with. But now I am venturing into the field of mythology. I should stop here.

7 Conclusion

In the Introduction I pointed out that the essays comprising this book derived their formal unity from being founded upon the conviction that certain fundamental philosophical problems could only be satisfactorily understood in relation to central religious themes and ideas, and conversely. It is in this sense that these essays are essays in the philosophy of religion. But do these essays also possess a *material* unity of doctrine, standpoint, etc.? I believe they do. I should like in this Conclusion to spell this out.

There is a philosophical attitude which expresses itself in the following, and related, forms of thoughts: 'This world is all that there is', 'This life of mine, which is terminated by my death, is all that there is of "me" ', and so on. A rejection of this attitude, which could be called the 'immanentist' metaphysical attitude, is a presupposition of all the essays of this book. This attitude is rejected implicitly in this book not on the ground that it expresses a verifiably false philosophical position, but on the ground of its essential unintelligibility.

Consider the statement or thought 'This world is all that there is'. The immanentist thrust of this thought or statement derives from the use of the demonstrative *This*. But this use is illegitimate. Consider what the word 'world' must mean in the above thought. It can only mean 'the totality or system of all actual and possible states of affairs'. The totality or system of all actual and possible states of affairs must be inclusive of all states of affairs, including the state of affairs constituted by the would-be demonstrative identification of such a totality. But strictly there can be no intelligible demonstrative identification or acknowledgement of 'the world'. For such an identification of the world to be possible, one would have to be 'outside' the world. But then 'the world' would not be all-inclusive, it would not be inclusive of the state of affairs constituted by one's existence. Thus the thought '*This* world', which constitutes the logical heart of the immanentist 'world-view', is an illegitimate thought. The idea of 'the world', conceived as the totality or system of all actual and possible states of affairs, is the idea of that in relation to which nothing can be said or thought — not even a demonstrative thought can be thought in relation to it. The idea or notion of the world is a notion of the mystical — a notion of that about which nothing — logically nothing — can be said. (I have discussed this in Essay 5, 'The Mystical'.) I think the inexpressibility of monistic metaphysics has to do with the logical impossibility of saying anything about 'the world' conceived as an absolute totality. Types of current materialism are monistic in this sense, and they can only fallaciously endorse an immanentist vision of the world.

Suppose somebody construed the notion of 'the world' not as the notion of the totality of all actual and possible states of affairs, but as the notion of 'the world as we know it'. Could he be an immanentist in relation to the world, so conceived? Not if he is a scientist. As a scientist he would never be able to acquiesce in any given state of scientific knowledge of the fundamental physical character of the world. New scientific discoveries are always round the corner, and there is a continuous enrichment of the scientific world-view. But the scientist's non-immanentism is of what might be called a *horizontal* sort. He does not discover in the world, as it is scientifically grasped at any period of history, anything fundamentally self-discrepant which would prevent him from ascribing to the very *general* character of the world, as he sees it, an absolute, ultimate, status. But as a self-conscious human being he cannot ascribe to the world as it discloses itself to scientific inquiry an absolute, ultimate, status. In order to show this I would like to recall certain arguments which I have employed in Essay 4, entitled 'Theism, Non-theism, and Morality'.

I argued there that an examination of the structure of human self-consciousness reveals that every human being, in so far as he is self-conscious, logically necessarily regards himself as being minimally valuable, as deserving minimal care. Now a modern scientist, say an evolutionary scientist, must regard human beings, self-conscious human beings, as being products of evolving Nature. It is Nature which has fashioned such necessarily minimally self-valuing human beings. But it is the same Nature which sets human beings in environments and situations where they are not at all even minimally valued, and for no fault of theirs. This is the great 'betrayal' of man by Nature. (Suitable non-anthropocentric language can, with sufficient ingenuity, be supplied here, but that is not essential to the argument.) An evolutionary scientist may argue that this 'betrayal' is only apparent, that in fact it endows us with an enormous evolutionary advantage. The very fact that Nature does not unfailingly (to put it mildly) shield us from harm enables us to fall back more and more upon our own resources, upon 'one another', upon co-operative, social, modes of life. But can we in all honesty say that in moments of great crisis — when death and disability and despair stalk us — we are able to do anything adequate for one another? The great 'betrayal' of which I spoke may heighten species-consciousness, and sharpen the concept of humanity, but it can and does break the human spirit. What I called the horizontal non-immanentism of science — its open-mindedness — can only heighten this dilemma, it cannot overcome it. Scientific knowledge is certainly a gain, but not in ultimate self-confidence. There remains at the heart of Nature, as it discloses itself to evolutionary science, a fundamental self-discrepancy — the discrepancy which consists in the evolution of logically necessarily self-valuing human beings and their situation in a heartless material environment. The evolutionary humanist world-view — and I am assuming that it is a scientifically well-established view — is not really a view of a 'coherent' world at all. How can a self-discrepant world be a coherent world — how can it be a 'world' at all? And how can one be an immanentist in relation to *such* a world?

But I do not believe that we are entitled to infer from the above considerations that there must be, in additon to the strangely self-discrepant natural world — the world of evolutionary humanism — 'another', 'transcendent', world, where human self-consciousness is not frustratingly set in an uncaring — not even minimally caring — environment. But if one cannot be an immanentist in relation to the natural world, and if there are insuperable difficulties — as I believe there are — in the way of cognitively grasping any notion of 'transcendence', does this mean that the notion of transcendence is unavailable to human beings in any form? I want to answer this question by examining another expression of the immanentist world-view which I set out at the beginning of this Conclusion. I had stated that the immanentist position often expressed itself in the form of the following thought: 'This life of mine, which is terminated by my death, is all that there is of "me".'

Is the above thought a legitimate thought? The immanentist thrust of this thought derives from a certain inadequate mode of thinking the thoughts symbolised by such expressions as 'me' and 'mine'. In Essay 2, 'Soul', I argued that if I lay dying, slipping into what I would be constrained to take to be irreversible unconsciousness, the thoughts 'I' or 'me' would begin to cease to be available to me, because all thoughts would begin to cease to be available to me. And that in such a condition if I still wanted to be able to think the thoughts 'I' or 'me' or 'myself', I could do so only by invoking an omnipotent, caring, consciousness, who would 'resuscitate' my self-consciousness 'beyond death'. However inadequately comprehensible the notion of such a caring consciousness, and the notion of such a resuscitation, may be, I am constrained at the time of dying to invoke these notions in so far as I wish to to think the thoughts 'I' or 'me' or 'myself'. (I am talking about logical pressures here, not of what actually or inevitably happens.) If I am right here, then I cannot take a 'summing-up' view, an immanentist view, of my life when I contemplate my death. At the time of dying — whether this 'time' is actually or imaginatively suffered — the thought or fragment of thought symbolised by the expression 'my' would or could be available to me only via the thought of a resuscitation of self-consciousness which can be effected 'beyond death' only by an adequately caring consciousness, i.e. God, whose reality I can exploratorily-communicatively, although 'groundlessly', invoke. There is no logical illegitimacy involved in exploratorily-communicatively seeking, summoning, a communicative being in whose reality one has no 'grounds' for believing. A classic theistic prayer of the form 'God, let me not be annihilated!' would serve the ends of an exploratory-communicative summoning of God's help. Such a prayer would render discrepant my immanentist view of 'my life' or 'myself' coming to an end. And it would non-cognitively make available to me the category of transcendence. For in exploratorily-communicatively invoking God's help, I invoke the reality of a being who must be 'transcendent' of the self-discrepant character of the natural world. God cannot be conceived as harbouring self-discrepancy, i.e. as being grossly imperfect. (Not that subtle imperfections can be attributed to God.) The availability of the idea of God is such that I cannot see my life as an immanent totality, bracketed between my birth and death.

In Essay 4, 'Theism, Non-theism, and Morality', I argued that I am, like everybody else, under an obligation minimally to value all human beings. Now if you or he were dying or dead, I must at least try to *think* of you and him (and not merely *remember* you or him, call up memories of you and him) if I am to fulfil the obligation of minimal care towards you and him. I must seek to cast you and him as objects of a caring communicative attention, if I am to think of you and him as self-conscious. But I can do this only by, again, invoking an omnipotent and caring consciousness who resuscitates you 'beyond' death. Again

I cannot, except fallaciously, see your lives as immanent totalities, bracketed between birth and death.

Now I am aware that we lack cognitive clarity about the ideas of God's saving agency and the resuscitation of self-consciousness beyond death. In particular, the idea of a resuscitation of self-consciousness beyond death raises the following acute difficulty. *Where* is a resuscitated self-consciousness supposed to be *located*? We may talk science-fictionally or occultistically of 'planes' or 'dimensions' of existence in order to answer such a question. But there is no occultist physics or geometry which, as far as I know, meets even quite elementary demands of mathematical rigour; and so occultist language cannot really make intelligible such notions as the locatedness of a post-mortem self-consciousness. There is, however, an aspect of the idea of a resuscitation of self-consciousness beyond death which makes questions about the locatedness of such a self-consciousness seem irrelevant, and this fact makes the idea of a resuscitated self-consciousness more intelligibly available to us than it would be otherwise.

In the essay on 'Theism, Non-theism, and Morality', and also elsewhere in this book, I have introduced the idea of a resuscitation of self-consciousness beyond death in a special context. The death of a person does not release us from the obligation to at least minimally care for him (the notion of personality-annihilation is too obscure a notion to serve as a knock-down argument against saying this). And in order to care for a person we must at least *think* of him (as distinguished from merely remembering him). But how can we minimally caringly think of him except as being self-conscious? And how can we think of him as being self-conscious when, to all appearances, he has totally receded from self-consciousness? My suggestion was that we must think of the dead person as being *rendered* self-conscious by God's saving act of addressing him. Only an act of being addressed is capable of rendering one self-conscious *in the first instance*. (I have argued — see Essay 2 — that we are imaginatively able to sustain self-consciousness, but only because originally we were rendered self-conscious by being addressed by another or others.) Now for a dead person to be rendered self-conscious 'beyond death' he must — so the picture unfolds — be addressed by God, who alone has the power and love to accomplish such a 'second birth' of self-consciousness. Undoubtedly, picture-thinking is involved here, but I believe we are under an obligation to employ such a picture. Now when someone, A, is addressed by another, B, A is not *located* by B as being in such-and-such-a-place, in so-and-so-way, etc. This is because *in* addressing A, B does not *refer* to A (e.g. allude to his locatedness). So that, strictly, the idea of A being addressed by B does not essentially connect with any specifiable clarity about A's mode of locatedness. A is rendered self-conscious by B by means of a vocative appeal which becomes operative within A's resources for self-consciousness. There is no picture-thinking here. This is a fact, although indeed a mysterious fact, of our ordinary communicative experience.

Thus in forming the picture, or thinking the thought, of A being rendered self-conscious beyond death by God's vocative agency, we are under no pressure to think of A's mode of locatedness. God stirs A's potentiality for self-consciousness by addressing A, and A *comes forth*, is *called*, is rendered self-conscious.

No question about the locatedness of God can be a legitimate question. God is conceived as being omnipresent, he is not grounded exclusively in any one 'place'. The idea of God links up with our life and thought in innumerable ways. In this book I have emphasised that idea of God which forces itself upon us whenever we try to make sense of our moral obligation to do things which are humanly impossible — beyond our powers — to do. This idea is the idea of a being whom we *call upon*, at least exploratorily-communicatively, whenever we encounter, or acknowledge, our own utter helplessness. It is the idea of a communicative being, a being who can be addressed and who can also address. Thus the idea of a resuscitation of self-consciousness beyond death is the idea of God addressing the dead, summoning them from the innermost recesses of unconsciousness, and rendering them self--conscious, without the thought of the *locatedness* of the resuscitated beings intruding into the picture. The thought of a resuscitation of self-consciousness beyond death, and the thought of God, are certainly thoughts of 'transcendent' realities. Notwithstanding their cognitive unclearness, they are available to us, and not as mere fanciful pictures; they are available to us as pictures which interlock with undeniable features of our own ordinary human reality.

When we think of death and other crises of human life, and the need and obligation to invoke the reality of God in such crises, we are thinking of limit-situations. But it is not only in limit-situations that the notion of 'transcendence', in some form or other, becomes available to us. Consider our ordinary communicative situation. I argued in Essay 2, 'Soul', that when we think of one another as being in communicative contact with one another, we think of one another quite simply as one another — as you, she, or he — and not as beings of any *kind* whatever. In his communicative aspect, we think of a person as being unclassifiably unique — as being himself. Here, at the very centre of our ordinary commerce with one another, we have access to a notion of transcendence of the utmost purity. In thinking of you as being, quite simply, you, I think of you as one who 'transcends all classifications'. I do not, when I so think of you, think of you as being material, or mental, or subtle-material, or subtle-mental, etc., in nature, but quite simply as *you*. The powerful religious idea of man being created in the image of God becomes clarified in this context. The 'transcendence' of God is reflected in the uniqueness and unclassifiability of a person considered in his communicative mode of existence.

In Essay 6, 'The Miraculous', I argued that the intelligibility of our basic motor-sensory-perceptual-intellectual-imaginative capacities does not rest upon, or require, any causal knowledge. And that the actions — I called them non-instrumental actions — which flowed from these capacities were properly to be described as being 'miraculous' in character, because quite properly speaking they involved the bringing into being of something from 'nothing'. Now self-consciousness itself can be seen as a dynamic reality, throbbing with non-instrumental activity, the locus of non-instrumental activity, itself a self-sustaining non-instrumental imaginative act. (Arguments in Essay 2 would support this.) Seen in this mode, we cannot think of self-consciousness — of ourselves — as being derivative from any past 'conditions'. We should want to say that we come from *nothing*, thereby echoing the powerful religious idea that man is created by God out of nothing. Given the general availability of this picture, we can participate in the following thought or attitude: when we die, we do not return to some anterior condition of existence from which we are derivative, e.g. dust or ashes. This is because we cannot intelligibly conceive of our selves as being derivative from any *thing* or order of things in the past. Either we become *nothing*, or we go on along a path of spiritual growth.

But can we straightforwardly hope that there will be a post-mortem existence for us? I think not. A man may of course say 'I hope I'll survive death'. But in saying this or in thinking this thought he would not be doing very much more than wishing that death would not obliterate his personality. (I argued that this must be the case in Essay 3, 'Hoping and Wishing'.) And in wishing that death would not obliterate his personality, he would at least exploratorily-communicatively invoke the saving power of God. But can I say, 'There is hope that I will survive death'? I can't. There is no science of super-nature, or anything like a commonsense view of the 'other world' and its connection with this world, to enable me to adduce any sort of grounds for saying 'There is hope that I will survive death'. And this is a crucial point because locutions of the form 'There is hope that *p*' can be employed sincerely only when there are *some* grounds for thinking that *p*. Nor can I say 'I am hoping against hope that I will survive death', because this sort of hoping makes sense only when some sort of probabilistic computation of chances is possible. But in the case of hope of survival this does not make sense. There isn't available a framework of scientific theory or common experience in the context of which alone probabilistic computations can be made.

But surely, somebody may argue, can't we at least hope that the personalities of those who have died have not been obliterated? But the difficulty here is again the following. What does 'not having been obliterated' come to in terms of experiential or scientific understanding? And hoping is unavoidably embedded in such understanding, unavailable here. We can certainly *see* the dead *as* being vocatively identified by God and rendered self-conscious. And we are, I believe, under a moral obligation to see the dead in such a manner. But this is not the same thing as *hoping* that the dead have not suffered annihilation of personality. The picture here is not embedded in any experiential or scientific understanding of the nature of things, but on the nature of 'ourselves' — on our need and obligation, at least exploratorily-communicatively, to invoke the reality of an all-caring consciousness. And as far as we, the living, are concerned, we can only pray to God that we may survive death, or exploratorily-communicatively invoke God's saving agency. I must confess my inability to see how the crucial religious idea of hope of an after-life, etc., can be available to an uncommitted seeker after the wisdom of religious language.

But perhaps I have misunderstood the spirit of theistic hoping. Perhaps what I have failed to grasp is the fact that the chief objects of theistic hoping are *miraculous* in character. Take the idea of survival. The availability, intelligibility, of the idea of survival does not derive from and understanding, physical or metaphysical, that we possess of the nature of things. It derives from the availability, intelligibility, of the idea of God miraculously resuscitating the dead by addressing them, resuscitating their self-consciousness by summoning them, calling them forth. The theist has faith in the reality of God, and he consequently is able to hope that such a miracle will take place, has taken place, etc. And this kind of *hope*, by reason of its being a hope for the miraculous (not to be confused with 'the extremely unlikely'), does not, and cannot, require to be embedded in experiential and scientific understanding. I failed to take into account this kind of hoping in Essay 3 on 'Hoping and Wishing'. The theistic hope that there will be a meeting with loved ones beyond death is similarly a hope that God will miraculously form a community, not by bringing together its members from spatiotemporally specifiable 'places', but by making them miraculously communicatively available to one another. So is the hope that there will be opportunities for spiritual growth beyond death. This connects with the idea of a miraculous transfiguration of environments — again an idea which does not owe its intelligibility to experiential or scientific understanding.

The non-theist does not *believe* in the existence of God. But the availability of the idea of God makes it possible for him to exploratorily-communicatively seek God, and as a consequence of this it makes it possible for him to seek theistic hope. This is the general mode of availability of theistic hope.

Who is a theist? A theist is a person who is able, with conviction, to say or think the following sorts of things — 'God is real', 'We will survive death through God's miraculous saving agency', 'We will never cease to have opportunities for spiritual growth', and so on. He may or may not be able to claim to establish by argument the reasonableness of his words and thoughts. But his faith *is* the availability to him of these words and thoughts as forms of conviction. I have not anywhere in this book attempted to uncover the structure of this form of conviction, the structure of theistic consciousness. But I have made attempts to gain an insight into the structure of a sort of non-theistic consciousness. Such a consciousness is the consciousness of a person whose wishes, strong wishes, correspond to the objects of many of the theist's convictions. The kind of non-theist I have in mind wishes that he and others would not be obliterated by death; that possibilities of spiritual growth would always be available to him and others; that the seeming futility and evil of suffering in the world, past and present, would somehow be able to be seen as not constituting an ultimate, irremediable, irrationality; and so on. And the sort of person I am thinking of doesn't merely strongly entertain wishes of the above sort, he feels he is under a moral obligation to entertain them. How close is such a person to theism?

The answer to the above question depends very much on the nature of human wishing. In Essay 3, 'Hoping and Wishing', I suggested an analysis of acts of wishing which would yield the following interpretations of wishes of the above kind. My wish that I and others would not be obliterated by death necessarily involves my thinking the following thought: 'If anybody is willing and able to save me and others from death, let him do so!' Now this thought cannot be a mere private agitation of my mind. It is an imperatival thought and even in an unverbalised form it demands for itself the status of a piece of would-be communication. It amounts to exploratorily-communicatively addressing, invoking, an appropriate communicative agency. It is 'exploratory' communication because I do not *know* whether or not there is a communicative agency who is 'appropriate' with respect to the imperatival thought I exploratorily 'throw out'. But theists maintain that God *is*, by definition, just the sort of communicative agency I invoke in thought. He can 'hear' our innermost thoughts — so the fact of my imperatival thought being non-verbalised need not prevent me from regarding it as a piece of would-be communication. And God — so the theistic definition unfolds — is just the being who is able and willing to save us from death. Thus my imperatival thought, 'If anybody is able and willing to save me and others from the annihilatory power of death, let him do so!', can be legitimately regarded as an explora-tory-communicative invocation of God.

The theistic definition of God also contains the idea that God would ensure that there would be possibilities of growth for men beyond death, and that he would make intelligible to us the apparent chaos and evil of the world and the waste of human and animal lives and so on. So my wish that men would have opportunities for spiritual growth beyond death could be regarded as necessarily involving the following thought: 'If anybody is able and willing to ensure that there would be possibilities of spiritual growth beyond death, let him do so!' And this thought could be legitimately regarded as exploratorily-communicatively addressed to God, or sought to be addressed to God. Similarly, the wish that the chaos and evil of the world and human and animal life be made intelligible can be regarded as necessarily involving the thought, 'If anybody is able and willing to make intel- ligible the apparent chaos and evil of the world, etc., let him do so!' And this thought could be regarded as an exploratory-communication addressed to God, or sought to be addressed to God. So the kind of non-theist I have been thinking of can be justly described as seeking God by seeking to address him. He may not of course realise this, but if the philosophical arguments of this book have any validity, he could be persuaded to accept as just such a description of him. Now I have often said in this book that I do not know what God's mode of response must be like to an exploratory-communicative search for him. But in a way we do know. God's mode of response to the non-theist's exploratory search for him must be the *gift of faith*. I do not think, notwithstanding the great attrac- tiveness of St Anselm's *Proslogion*, that this gift could be the gift of a clinching philosophical argument. It could, instead, be the gift of a new way or new ways of looking at the world and ourselves. It could, for instance, be the gift of an ability to see self-consciousness as sustained not merely by an imaginatively posited consciousness, as I have argued in this book, but by a *real* caring presence, the presence of God. The conviction could grow that in so far as self-consciousness retains an inner peace and lucidity,

God does not let go of one, abandon one, at all. It could be the gift of an ability to see spiritual capacities in the most wretched of human beings. The conviction could grow that their self-consciousness too is sustained by God. The gift of faith could be the gift of an ability to see in the order and beauty and explicability of the world *not* conclusive evidence of divine creation, but something which is *so* unexpected in a morally self-discrepant world that it could only be regarded as a surrealist intervention of God in the world. Perhaps Simone Weil had something like this in mind when she wrote that to ignore the beauty of the world is the greatest crime of ingratitude imaginable. And perhaps it was something like this which led Gabriel Marcel to exclaim, 'Who knows what surprises await us?'

But now I am trying to do what I have not so far done at all in this book, i.e. examine the structure of theistic conviction. All I want to say is that God's mode of response to the non-theist's exploratory-communicative search for him may be the gift, in one or another of a variety of simple and complex forms, of theistic faith itself. I want to say this because I do not want to convey the impression that when I talk of an exploratory-communicative invocation of God by someone, I have in mind the possibility of an ordinary sort of 'speech-act' emanating from God.

What then has been the general theme of this book of essays? There are two general themes. One is the availability of religious ideas. A whole range of religious ideas — the ideas of soul, immortality, God, prayer, the mystical, the miraculous, and so on — are available to human beings outside a context of actual religious or theistic belief. Admission of these ideas into one's conceptual framework does not commit one to religious belief, but it does expose the unintelligibility of the immanentist view of the world. As I tried to point out earlier in this 'Conclusion', a variety of notions of 'transcendence' are available to the uncommitted philosophical imagination.

The other theme is that of morality. I have argued —

and this is a recurrent theme of the book — that an adequate analysis of the structure of human self-consciousness reveals universally applicable principles of morality. Morality does not stand in need of 'transcendental' support. However, in limit-situations, such as in the face of death and other kinds of humanly unredeemable suffering and loss, human beings are under logical pressure to invoke the reality of God, at least exploratorily-communicatively. It is at this point that the theistic and the non-theistic human consciousness come close together, upsetting many barriers that divide humanity into believers and non-believers. I should have liked to compare the non-theistic and theistic human consciousness more fully, but I have a very poor insight into the actual structure of theistic conviction. Consequently, my treatment of this theme in this book is very incomplete and inadequate. Indeed, I am aware that quite a lot of what I have written in this book is extremely tentative and exploratory. I only wish it were less unsatisfactorily so. However, I should like to hope that these essays indicate at least some fresh approaches to certain quite old worries in the philosophy of religion.

Index